AN UNBELIEVABLE TRUE STORY OF FAITH & LOVE

THE
MESSENGER

How do you define a miracle?

ROBERT CLANCY

FOREWORD BY SHEA VAUGHN

AN UNBELIEVABLE TRUE STORY OF FAITH & LOVE

THE
MESSENGER

By Robert Clancy

Foreword by Shea Vaughn

Mohawk Street Press
New York

FIRST EDITION

Cataloging-in-Publication Data

Clancy, Robert Steven

The Messenger

p.cm.

Summary: The Messenger is a real-life story of tragedy to triumph and sacrifice to redemption; the kind of story that inspires and gives hope.

[1. Self-Help – Inspirational 2. Angels 3. Spiritual
4. Motivational 5. Christianity 6. Faith]

ISBN: 978-0-9859395-5-7

Library of Congress Catalog-in-Publication data available upon request.

Cover Design and Layout: Neil Wright / Spiral Design Studio, LLC

www.SpiralDesign.com

ROBERT CLANCY

DEDICATION

For my precious wife Lauren,
my wonderful son Sean,
and my angel daughter Ramona.
I will forever love you with all my heart.
To God and His angels...
I will forever cherish the precious gifts
you bestowed upon my soul to
share with the world.

"For it is written, He shall give his angels charge over thee, to keep thee."

~ Luke 4:10 ~

CONTENTS

"Release your fears and worries, for the trials and tribulations you've endured were only meant to show you how resilient your precious soul is. Allow love to be the peace-filled eye of every one of life's hurricanes."

— *Robert Clancy*

ROBERT CLANCY

CONTENTS

ROBERT CLANCY

PRAISE

"What a journey! *The Messenger* is a wonderfully written and touching story that beautifully takes you through the trials of the human condition to the divine. In this precious book, Robert Clancy illustrates you are never alone, you're always in God's hands, and heaven is real. I know Robert and his amazing back story and I'm thrilled he's now sharing it with the world. Robert is a true gift. Such an inspiring read!"

— **Dr. Joe Vitale**, *Bestselling Author, and Featured Teacher from The Secret*

"So uplifting! In *The Messenger*, Robert Clancy immerses you into his divinely inspired world — a wonderful place filled with radiant light and angelic love. It's clear that not only has Robert been on a divinely guided path, but he shows you that we all are—it's just up to us to follow it as he reveals to you. Robert is real, transparent, and open in his writing; it's one of the greatest gifts an author can give you."

— **Dee Wallace**, *Actress, Bestselling Author, Healer and Speaker*

"*The Messenger* will take you on a beautiful and inspiring journey of the heart. Robert Clancy's riveting story offers a powerful healing message of hope and faith."

— **Marci Shimoff**, *New York Times Bestselling Author of Happy for No Reason and Love for No Reason*

15

"Robert's story moved me to tears—tears of pure joy. If there are such things as earth angels, you will come to know one and his amazing journey when you read this book. There are so many inspiring moments in this book that touched more than just my heart; they touched my soul. I love, love, love this book! This is a must-read!"

— **Lisa Winston**, *International Bestselling Author, TV Host, Producer, and Inspirational Speaker*

"*The Messenger* is a wonderfully written hero's journey of enlightenment, self-discovery, and ultimately, how to find peace among the chaos of life. This book has exactly what the documentary Finding Joe describes for every epic story. When you walk your true path and slay your dragons, you may discover that the holy grail you seek has always been inside you."

— **Teresa de Grosbois**, *#1 International Bestselling Author of Mass Influence*

"Robert Clancy's *The Messenger* is a story of love and hope. It is an amazing story of faith, transforming a young man into a major spiritual leader. If you don't believe in angels now, you will after reading this book. What the world needs now is a sign that there is something more, that each of us can achieve our dreams and goals. The Messenger will show you everything you desire is yours for the asking when you hold onto faith. You won't be able to put this down!"

—**Mark Alyn**, *Award-Winning Host and Executive Producer of Late Night Health Radio*

"It's rare to read a book that resonates so deeply with my Soul. The poignant moments shared in Robert's story touched me deeply. Uplifting is an understatement. This book takes you straight to heaven. The Messenger is pure, wondrous light-filled energy."

— **Valerie René Sheppard**, *International Bestselling Author of Living Happy to Be ME!*

"Robert Clancy's book, *The Messenger*, is about holding onto hope during your darkest night. This beautifully written story will show you how God holds you through all of life's trials and tribulations. I love how visceral and poignant his journey of compassion is. When beautiful souls like Robert follow their divine path to help others, it's abundantly clear that angels do indeed guide you."

— **Robin Jay**, *Award-winning Inspirational Filmmaker and Author*

"*The Messenger* is a beautifully written, entertaining, and engaging journey of faith. It will not only inspire you, but it will guide you never to lose hope. In this book, Robert shows you so beautifully that you are never alone. If you don't believe in angels, you will be after reading his story. Such an uplifting read!"

— **Daniel Gutierrez**, *Multiple Bestselling Author, International Speaker, and Mindful Leadership Expert*

"I believe *The Messenger* will become a spiritual classic. Robert Clancy has managed to tell a story, his story, and made it not only inspiring and enlightening, but life-affirming and life-changing. It conveys a message that will not only make you a better person, but the world a better place."

— **Servet Hasan**, *International Book Award Winner, Radio Host and Motivational Speaker.*

FOREWORD

By Shea Vaughn

The Messenger is based on the extraordinary true story of Robert (Bobby) Clancy who, at 19, experienced an incredible miracle that he kept secret for more than 30 years. This phenomenon not only radically transformed his bleak vision of the future, but forever re-characterized his life's purpose into something entirely divinely guided.

Robert is an accomplished technology entrepreneur, creative visionary, international bestselling author, dynamic speaker, awakened teacher, and a 6th-degree black belt martial arts instructor who lives in upstate New York with his lovely wife Lauren, and their son Sean.

Robert grew up in a loving, middle-class family in a typical suburban neighborhood. His father, John Clancy, served in World War II, married his sweetheart Margaret, and together they raised John Jr., Karen, David, and Robert. From an early age, his parents instilled the powers of leadership, love, kindness, volunteerism, and faith into his heart.

Robert, the youngest of his siblings, still lived at home when he began to experience a series of devastating events that left him struggling, feeling overwhelmed and lost. These unfortunate circumstances were the catalyst that started his downward spiral. To dull his intense emotional pain, he turned to drugs and drinking. Then, unexpectedly, amidst all of this turmoil, his girlfriend broke up with him and, feeling deserted, he found himself in an existential crisis, unable to function.

The Messenger is a real-life story of a man going from failure to success and sacrifice to redemption. It's the kind of story that inspires and gives hope. This journey is one of personal courage and divine guidance that teaches us how to change tragedy into triumph when we surrender to our true calling!

While doing a television interview, a colleague introduced me to Robert. When we met, I found his voice and words uplifting and exhilarating. I was thrilled when he invited me to be a guest on his television show, "The Mindset Reset Show" where I would also get to meet his soul-sister co-host, Lisa Winston. I said, "Of course!" and we all immediately became soul friends.

During my first meeting with Robert he shared his story with me. I listened deeply to the truth in his voice and cried. I was so grateful and moved by his beautiful words. He surprised me when he said, "I've kept my divine encounter a secret from almost everyone who knows me." He went on to tell me that he didn't even tell his father and siblings until 2012—the day his mother died. I was stunned. I knew immediately in my heart that his story needed to be shared with the world. Robert surprised and enlightened me when he said, "I feel that God may have brought us together so you could help me. People need to know heaven is real, angels exist, and God holds us all.

I'm ready to surrender to my truth." I paused and said, "If God put that in your heart, I'm all in!"

Robert's journey is an authentic, personal story that empowers you to never give up on yourself. Above all, it is a message about having faith, holding onto hope in your darkest hours, and defeating fear with love.

love + joy —

Shea

ROBERT CLANCY

ACKNOWLEDGEMENTS

"My family and friends are the feathers for my
wings. I can only soar the heavens on the love
and support they give me."

— *Robert Clancy*

The path to *The Messenger* was not created by pen to paper or keys typed into a screen, but by the many kind souls, kindred spirits and angels I've met along my life's highway.

I thank God and the universe for guiding me on my path to enlightenment.

I thank my wonderful parents, my brothers, John and Dave, and my sister Karen for being such an amazing, loving family. Without you, I would not be who I am. I love you all unconditionally.

Gratitude for my soul mother, Shea Vaughn, and my soul sister Lisa Winston. Thank you for seeing the light that is within me that I also recognize that is shining within your beautiful hearts.

Thanks to all of my precious friends and colleagues with a special shoutout to: Mark Alyn, Dr. Joe Vitale, David Wood,

Jeffrey Mallian, Dee Wallace, Teresa de Grosbois, Pam Bayne, Evana Valle, Valerie Rene Sheppard, Lisa Mininni, Scott Schilling, Sharon McRill, Sherri Richards, Catherine Saykaly-Stevens, Anna Pereira, Shari Alyse, Robin Jay, Servet Hasan, Kali Koester Nandi, Dr. Partha Nandi, Marci Shimoff, Jim Knox, Julie Massry-Knox, Nehme Frangie, Margaret Lynch Partyka, Gary Stewart, Daniel Gutierrez, Tamara Green, David Dachinger, Debbi Dachinger, Catherine Saykaly-Stevens, Eric Zuley, Denise Millett-Burkhardt, Tina Dietz, Liberty Forrest, Jo Davis, Lou Defelippo, Hugh O'Brian, the Poutre family, the Blasch family, the teams at WomanOnTV, eZway and all of my amazing colleagues and friends at Spiral Design, the Evolutionary Business Council, Chon-Ji Defensive Arts, The Wellness Universe, and the Hugh O'Brian Youth Foundation (HOBY).

Blessed to have childhood friends such as Jeff Krause, Ron Wachenheim, Ed Aidalla, Joe Corrigan, Jaydene Miner-Drew, Tony Pallone, Joe Pallone, Bill Ketzer, Pat Poutre, Greg Henzel, and Mike Normandin.

Finally, I thank you for reading this book. Share your kindness and love with the world!

PROLOGUE

*"Faith, love, and death are all parts of life.
The differences among them are that faith
carries us through life, death ends our life,
and love transcends it."*

— Robert Clancy

Does every season you go through in life serve a higher purpose—from the depths of your worst imaginable despair to the happiest moment of your life?

What if everything you've ever experienced is orchestrated—no coincidences, no chance encounters, and no mistakes—only truth— truth of who you are and everything you were ever meant to be?

Are God, Heaven, and His angels for real?

What if you knew beyond a shadow of a doubt that God exists?

How would you live the rest of your days if you were shown definitive proof of Heaven?

How would you change?

It's not that God gives you more than you can handle in life; it's that you discover His grace in what you overcome. I know. I've been there.

Not all of my days were dark, though...in fact, most of my life was wrapped in divine love. I've always been on this path. It has always been up to me to choose to walk it with faith.

When I've thought deeply about the word "belief," I discovered that everything about it is contained within the action of merely doing it—no proof. Your pure faith is the one thing that allows you to possess it unquestionably.

For more than half my life, I've kept a secret from almost everyone who has known me—a profoundly spiritual, life-altering divine encounter.

When my mother passed away a few years ago, there was an additional layer of sadness in my soul because I never shared anything about this celestial encounter with her. I've kept this secret for two reasons: partially to avoid being judged and, to some extent, because it's been a gift I've held close in my heart.

Only God knows, with total absolution, the truth of what I am about to share with you.

I was nineteen years old, and my whole life was falling apart at the seams. I was disheveled. I hadn't slept well in weeks. Most nights, I was so impaired that I struggled just to get home.

The night I was standing firmly on rock bottom, I stumbled into my house. As I sneaked past my father, who was asleep on the couch, I caught a blurry glimpse of my mother at the kitchen table. She was watching the news on a small television that sat next to the counter. She was solemnly engrossed and didn't notice me. I didn't want her to.

I wanted to disappear from reality. I didn't care if I lived or died.

When I stumbled into my bedroom, a picture of my ex-girlfriend greeted me. Weeks had passed since our relationship had unraveled along with my heart. I thrashed the frame onto the floor. A funeral mass card for one of my friends was another unwelcomed guest. I crumpled it up and threw it against the wall hitting a cross that hung there — all reminders of what I was trying to escape—pain. I was so alone in my anguish.

I raised my fists to God. "Why?"

As tears flowed down my cheeks, I rummaged through my dresser, pulled out a prescription medicine bottle, and a small bottle of liquor I'd hidden there. I popped some of the pills with a good swig from the bottle. The deadly cocktail filled my belly, and I flopped onto my bed in a dazed heap.

My aching heart begged. "I hate my life. Just make this pain inside me go away."

There it is, my darkest day. The day I stopped caring about everything. The day I gave up on hope.

In time I learned the darkness could never rule the light. The hopeless night only inspires the dawn's light to be that much brighter. Light creates the dark, and it's only ever a shadow. When you are mired in the shadows of that despair, there is always a higher light source surrounding you. You just need to turn around to see it.

In that desolate chasm, I found one precious thing—it takes but a single ray of hope to defeat that darkness. You just have to have enough faith to hold onto it.

ONE

EROS

"Love may be a simple word, yet
it simply means everything."

—Robert Clancy

What is your earliest memory of love? When was the first time you understood what it was? Was it in your mother's gracious smile? Were you born predisposed to it, or is it learned while you make your journey through life? I know now I've always known what love is, and it's more beautiful than you could ever imagine.

There I was, a content wide-eyed brown-eyed baby boy standing in my crib pointing at a closed door trying to get my mother's attention. She is the very first conscious memory I have, and it was long before I could speak. She always greeted me with her precious smile—a glimmering light that never left her face. The only thing that stole her smile for a brief time was her cancer diagnosis toward the end of her life. Even so, she still managed to pull through it with her smile intact.

"You little stinker! You're supposed to be taking your nap."

She looked so intently into my eyes. I could feel her heart. The light I felt radiating from her was unconditional love, and it was beautiful. I never wanted this feeling to leave me, but it seemed to happen the minute she left the room. I remember being frustrated because I couldn't tell her I loved her. I wanted her to stay with me.

You are born with everything necessary to communicate love with the greatest instrument you possess —your heart. It's all I had to work with and all I ever needed.

At three years old, my family moved into the neighborhood that would shape my very existence. On the front steps of our suburban split-level ranch house, I sat with a young girl named Dana from my neighborhood. I remember how kind her heart seemed. Our black and white tabby cat named Mittens was perched on her lap. As she gently stroked him, his purring mixed with the warm summer breeze that wrapped us in its warmth.

I handed her a wildflower I'd picked from our yard. As she smelled it, her eyes met mine, and a small smile flowed across her lips.

When I think back upon this moment, I knew then that love and kindness are connected just as your heart is connected to the entire universe. This divine prose is written into the very fiber of your being. In this simple exchange of kindness, a celestial bridge was formed. I was ready to cross this expanse into everything life ahead of me had to offer. I had to experience everything that is love.

I quickly learned there is the kind of love you discover when two hearts meet, but there is also a divine love that unlocks the entire universe within your heart—the one your soul speaks so fluently, but you seem to forget the second you're born. I know I never lost this heavenly memory.

As you travel down your life's path, you may never see the grand picture God has painted for you because you're always standing on that canvas. There are times when all you see around you is darkness, and that picture becomes blurry or unclear. How can that be? It's masked with fear, doubt, and worry. I've learned that you just need to have enough faith and hope to know this image, and the message it holds is beautiful. It's all about how you frame that image. Sometimes that frame can be even more beautiful than the picture it contains.

How would you change if you were shown the entire painting God made of you? How would you frame it?

TWO
EXODUS

*"There are persons so radiant, so genial, so kind, so
pleasure bearing, that you instinctively feel their
presence that they do you good, whose coming into
a room is like the bringing of a lamp there."*
—Henry Ward Beecher

I believe a reverence for others and a sense of community comes from your family, but it also comes from the kindred spirits you meet along the way. My first act of compassion for others was at age six. I was given this precious opportunity. A gift from a fantastic kindred spirit I'd met by chance. It was not a coincidence—it was a *God-incidence*.

It was July of 1971, and I was six years old getting ready for the biggest adventure of my life. We were all on our way to a beautiful vacation in Jamaica. My father, a decorated World War II veteran, was anxiously standing near the open trunk of our 1969 Rambler rounding us all up.

"Come on, Karen...will ya get a move on?"

My sister returned a flustered glance while she dragged her

heavier than average luggage bag to the trunk.

My father was in military time. "Did you ever hear the phrase 'travel lightly'?"

"A girl has needs, Pop," she sighed.

He pushed his dark-rimmed glasses back onto the bridge of his nose, looked nervously at his watch and shook his head. His gaze then beamed at the open front door of our house.

"Marge! We really gotta get going here...our flight leaves in an hour. Did you lock the screen door to the back porch?"

A muffled voice emitted from the doorway.

"I locked it *twice, honey!*"

My mother looked like Marlo Thomas. She was a beautician who was always put together. She had a salon in the basement of our house where she doted on the neighborhood ladies. She emerged from the front door dressed to the nines toting a large hat bag.

"Relax, dear. This is the last one. The house will be just fine, we'll be fine, and it will all be here when we get back."

As I climbed into the backseat of the car, my older brother David took a stow-away G.I. Joe out from behind his back and slipped it into a small luggage case. Dave was a straight-haired sandy blond, with blue eyes and a light complexion that exuded his Irish heritage. His stocky build made him look older than his actual age.

"Shhhh! I have some other stuff in there, too. It's in the G.I. Joe duffel bag."

I giggled.

My sister slumped into the back seat and rolled her eyes at the sight of the G.I. Joe. "Seriously? Mom! Do I have to spend the next two weeks babysitting these two? Can't I just stay home and hang out with my friends? Like when you and Pop went away for that long weekend?"

"Now, now. You'll make some new friends in Jamaica. You'll see. Did you grab the bag packed with all of Bobby's new clothes?" my mother asked as she cramped my sister even more with the hat bag.

She put her sunglasses on and tried to tune us out. "That's why I can barely fit back here along with these two. I love 'em, but not that much!"

I was just excited to be flying. I wanted to know what it was like to be that close to heaven.

"Mommy, when we go in the airplane, will I get to see angels sitting on the clouds?"

My mother beamed at me.

"I'm not sure about angels, but you'll be closer to heaven than you are now. That's for sure, honey."

The car trunk closed with a thud. My father hopped into the driver's seat and surveyed our faces.

"What? Did I miss something?"

My mother always knew how to handle him—a little bit of humor and a whole lotta love. "The only thing we might be missin' is our flight, dear. I love ya to bits, but let's get a move on.

We've got a vacation to be getting to!"

He returned a stink-eye.

"Well...go on...start the car already," she commanded with her ever-present smile.

There was anticipation exuding from the car. No one could have imagined how this trip would change us as a family or shape me as a person.

A few hours later, I was looking intently through the window of the plane at the billowing clouds below. A Jamaican female flight attendant smiling ear-to-ear stopped to clip a gold wings pin to my jacket.

"And who might we have here who just earned his wings like our captain?"

My eyes grew wide at the sight of the pin. "Whoa! I got a captain's pin!" I sat up proudly in my seat.

"Looks like you got him all wide-eyed and bushy-tailed. This little stinker is Bobby," my mother gleamed.

The flight attendant's smile grew a bit wider with my enthusiasm. "Is this his first time on a jet plane?"

"It's his first time, alright. He's been glued to the window looking for angels the whole flight."

I got a wink and a nod from the flight attendant. "Oh... they're out for sure. They're always watchin' over me, and they're watchin' over you too." She pointed to her heart. "You're gonna have so much fun on my beautiful island! The ocean is made from emeralds and sapphires, and the mountains in

Jamaica reach right into heaven."

"You're *Jah-nay-can*? I never met a *Jahnaycan* before."

"I'm *Jamaican*, alright, and you'll meet plenty more of my beautiful people when you get there." As the words left her lips, she paused to contemplate. "But I moved to Miami, Florida a few years ago. That's my new home. I'm afraid my island only has a home in my heart now."

She crossed her hands over her heart, and I touched the pin covering mine. There are people who are so wonderfully kind that merely being in their presence warms your heart like a beautiful sunrise. You always know when you're in the presence of this kind of light. As she headed down the aisle, she turned to share another smile and a wink with me. I can still see her smile on my heart to this day.

"She's very pretty mommy, and she's lucky...she gets to work close to heaven. I'll get to be an angel one day...right?"

My mother pulled me in for a hug. "You'll always be my little angel."

What you see in the mirror is a pure reflection of what surrounds you. What you see in the hearts of others is love's reflection of everything in the entire universe. Where your heart goes, your feet will most certainly follow, but more importantly, your soul will find a home.

THREE
STRANGERS IN A STRANGE LAND

"Be strong and of a good courage, fear not, nor be afraid of them: for the LORD thy God, he it is that doth go with thee; he will not fail thee, nor forsake thee."
—*Deuteronomy 31:6*

Do you become unsettled when you're not in your comfortable and familiar surroundings? Whenever I feel lost in those shadows, I've found that love is the light that can be found in the center of any darkness—it's the angelic beacon that will always help you find your way home.

Of all the places you'll ever go in life, there's none as important as the place you take others when you carry them deep within the preciousness of your heart.

My nose was firmly planted against the window of the plane as we taxied to the terminal of a small Jamaican airport. A grounds crew quickly moved in to attach stairs to plane, and the passengers began spilling out. My father was the first in our group to emerge from the aircraft. He carefully surveyed the surroundings as he always did. He quickly noticed the numerous exotically dressed Jamaican people and colorful tourists gathered around the front of the main terminal.

"The way we're dressed, we're all gonna stick out like a sore thumb here."

"Now, now, John. Don't we always stand out as a beautiful family?"

He pointed at the welcome center of the airport. "Meet me over there with the kids. I'll get the rest of our bags and see if I can hire a taxi to get us to our cottage—I hope. You know how traveling gets me on edge.

"We'll all be just fine, dear," she said.

We pooled up together at the curb of the welcome center as my father instructed, and waited for him. I began drinking in the beauty of this strange place. A Jamaican kettledrum band performed a Reggae song nearby. All of the band members were wearing brightly colored floral shirts. Exotic birds flew in and out of the palm trees. I loved all of the strange sights, sounds, and people.

My father emerged from the terminal carrying two large luggage bags. "They said to wait out front here, and a driver will find us."

As soon as those words left my father's lips, an imposing, muscular dark-skinned Jamaican man, approached us. He was dressed in a white, official-looking, short-sleeved uniform with black shoes and a white sailor's hat. His deep voice came with an equally thick Jamaican accent.

"Welcome to Jamaica, man! You folks be needin' a ride? I'm one of the finest drivers on the *whole island*."

My father hesitantly sized him up and handed him our resort brochure. "Sure thing, buddy. Can you get us to this resort?"

The man placed his hand on my father's shoulder in an attempt to comfort him. "No problem, man. My name is Dajuan. It means God is gracious and merciful—and He sure is. Let me get your bags, and you'll be there in no time at all."

My father relaxed a bit as Dajuan took off his hat, wiped the sweat from his brow, and knelt next to me. "Hey, little man. Is this your first time in Jamaica?"

"Mister, this is my first time *anywhere*."

A deep laugh bellowed from Dajuan. "Well then...you are in for quite an adventure, my friend. My beautiful island is filled with magic. Enjoy all you discover here. If you see a little yellow bird while you're here, it means the spirits are with you. Wink at it, and it will bring you good luck." He reassured me with a wink and a smile.

"Now let's be gettin' you on your way—everybody in the car. I'll be takin' you on the scenic route to your resort village. I call it the *Dajuan Special Tour*, and it's no extra charge for you fine folks."

As we got underway, exotic people and scenery splashed across my eyes. My brother pointed out various discoveries along the route, such as bananas and coconuts hanging from the trees.

I was amazed. "Whoa! Look at those!"

The only place I'd ever seen fruit was in a grocery store bin.

It was about thirty minutes into the journey when Dajaun pointed to a large white manor house. His tone turned ominous.

"Now we go past the White Witch of Rose Hall's house. My mother dun told me never to go there. There are bad spirits in that evil place." He turned our attention to a group of palm trees centered in a field. "They say she murdered all her husbands for money and buried them there. If you come here at midnight, you will see her walking the grounds in her white gown."

My mother shuddered at the thought and grabbed my father's shoulder. "Ooooh, Johnny. I don't like this."

Dajaun held up a small pouch and shook it. "That's why I carry jasmine with me...to ward off the evil spirits."

My sister slid deeper into her seat. "I'm gettin' creeped out here."

"Relax. It's just old wives' tales," my father said in his ever-confident matter of fact tone.

My sister quickly flashed a tourist brochure. "No, it's not! Look! It says so right here."

I looked curiously at the group of sinister looking palm trees as the car passed them.

My brother teased. "Maybe I'll bring you back here at midnight, Shrimp, and let that witch get you."

I was having no part of this. "Mommy! Make him stop!"

"David! Stop scaring him, or you'll be the one with him stayin' up all night with the lights on," my mother scolded.

My father made a feeble attempt to grab the reins of this runaway cart. "Can everybody just calm down?"

A short time later, the taxi suddenly came to a screeching halt on a dusty dirt road in the middle of a large field laden with grass taller than corn stalks. Dajuan turned off the car engine, flung his door open, hopped out, and pulled a large machete out from under his seat. He held up the blade for all of us to see. It glistened in the sunlight alongside the bright white teeth of his smile. As quickly as he exited the car, he disappeared into the field. Panic washed over the car like a fast-moving rainstorm.

My mother's head was spinning like a top. "Oh dear! What's he doing?"

"I lost him in the weeds. He might be getting others. I've heard about bandits on these islands who prey on tourists. I think he set us up! Dammit, Marge! I should have trusted my gut."

"What do we do?"

My family was in full five-alarm fear mode—everyone except me. I just sat there looking contently at the beauty of the field.

My sister grabbed the car door handle as the color ran from her face. "My life is over, and it hasn't even started yet. I'm gonna make a run for it!"

"Hush, Karen! Your father is..."

"Everybody just keep quiet and hold still. I'll handle any trouble. Just give me a minute to think...and...uh..."

Dajuan suddenly emerged from the field, holding up a clump of freshly cut grass in one hand and his machete in the other. He poked the grass stalks over the seat toward my brother and me.

"For the children, the freshest sugarcane in all of Jamaica. You don't eat it—you just chew on it. Enjoy, little ones!"

As my mother shed a sigh of relief, I smiled at Dajuan. "My mommy and daddy thought you were a bad man, but I knew you weren't."

My brother poked me. "Shhhh. Don't tell him that."

The color in my mother's face went from white to cherry red. "Well, with the machete and island bandits...we thought you were...you know...a..."

Dajuan stowed his machete back under the driver's seat and hopped into the car. "Ma'am. I assure you I'm a lover, not a killer, and there are no bandits." He looked over his shoulder and winked at me. "What have your imaginations been gettin' you to?"

Dajuan shook his head, rolled his eyes, and started the car. As he took off his hat to wipe the sweat from his brow again. "Now...about gettin' you folks back to startin' your vacation."

"...and opening our minds. *Right John?*" My mother gave her staple, "I told you so" look to my father.

The car erupted in laughter.

44

When life seems to be taking you for a ride, know that divine love will always ultimately be the final destination. Trust in the lessons of the journey. Believe in the truth discovered in your purpose. There are good people in our world—more than you'll ever be able to count. Every time you encounter one, celebrate the beauty of that exchange. I guarantee you that you will be in celebration every day of your life. Believe in yourself, for you are part of something greater. Believe in this greatness, for it is everything you are and everything you've always been.

Happiness is always in your hands. You cannot climb a mountain by continuously running away from it. The first step to conquering your fears is to face them. The views are always spectacular at all the summits of life.

We all learned a lesson of the heart that day.

FOUR
KINDRED SPIRITS

*"If there is a poor man among your brothers in any
of the towns of the land that the Lord your God is
giving you, do not be hardhearted or tightfisted
toward your poor brother. There will always be poor
people in the land. Therefore I command you to be
openhanded toward your brothers and toward the
poor and needy in your land."*

—Deuteronomy 15:7, 11

There are special moments that I've labeled *soul hitches* that can occur unexpectedly during everyday encounters. In fact, you can hitch a ride on someone's inner spirit by keeping yourself open to receiving it.

So what exactly is a *soul hitch*? It's any interaction—large or small—that changes how you view your life, your calling, or that guides you profoundly toward it. A *soul hitch* could come from a chance run-in with a stranger, from an intimate conversation with a family member, or a breakthrough moment with a friend. It's a soul connection where you open your heart fully to somebody's very essence. It can alter something in your thoughts, or it can change the course of your life and quite possibly save it. A piece of the other person stays with you. Their light resonates with your spirit for the rest of your days.

You're always driving down life's highway, en route to your life's purpose. And you have interruptions in that journey when you exit this road. Often, though, those exits take you off your enlightened path and into despair. I know people who have taken those exits who've never returned. The *soul hitches* you encounter are life's little reminders that you're driving too fast, that you need to see things differently, or that you need a critical message that guides you toward your real purpose. These guides are there to prevent you from exiting—to revitalize your soul and give you the strength and resolve to keep going.

During our stay in Jamaica, I came close to losing my life—not once but twice—and not just my life was spared, but also my soul. This trip was no ordinary vacation. This experience was the first profound step of my spiritual awakening.

⁓❀⁓❀⁓❀⁓

As we gathered our luggage in front of the resort, my father paid Dajuan and shook his hand. Dajuan drove off with a wide smile. I noticed a change in my father's posture after the exchange. He took a patriarchal position in front of us.

"It's not easy for me to drop my guard. I've seen the worst people can do to each other in this world, but your mother is right—I guess we'll have to keep an open mind while we're here."

My mother rubbed his back to comfort him. "I know, dear...I

know the war has always had you on edge, but these are good people here. Let's see what we find in their hearts."

My father's wartime service affected him for his entire life. Even in the last days of his life, after a debilitating stroke took his mobility, the staff at his nursing home would occasionally find him on the floor of his room. He'd roll out of his bed during nightmares. When I asked his about it, he said, "I was dodging German 88mm rounds and mortars. When you've been through something like a war, it will never leave you." He carried that to the end.

The next morning, my brother and I were walking on a palm-tree-lined, paved pathway. Numerous six-inch holes dotted the surrounding landscape. I was curiously taking them in. "Davey! What are all those holes for? It looks like moon craters."

"I dunno. Let's check 'em out. Maybe they have large chipmunks here or something."

As we approached one of the holes, a giant red Jamaican crab popped out of it. Its claws extended menacingly toward me. I screamed bloody murder and jumped behind my brother. As much as he teased me, my brother was always my protector. "Ahhhhhhhhhhh!!!!! Don't let it get me!"

"Relax, doofus. It's just a crab. I think I can catch it. Quick! Grab a stick."

My brother prodded the crab with the branch until it firmly latched onto it. He proudly held up the otherworldly creature.

As he displayed the crab, he flashed me a devilish grin.

"Follow me."

Moments later, we were sitting contently next to each other on the bed in our cottage. We watched our sister go in and out of the bathroom a few times before she finally entered it, closing the door behind her.

"You two better be good while I take my shower...and don't go anywhere!"

"Oh... We're not budging an inch," we smugly retorted.

With the anticipation of a NASA control room crew, we listened for the water come on, and the shower curtain to open...4...3...2...1 ignition...blast off!!! A piercing screech immediately followed a sudden thumping commotion emanated from the bathroom.

She ran past us and out of the cottage clasping only a towel to her body. "I really hate you two...and I'm telling Mom and Pop about this too!"

My brother and I still snicker to this day at the spectacle we created. Life was good. We were good. After all, if you're not having fun, what's the point of it all? Laughter is life's melody, meant to be performed with all your heart. Laughter heals, and smiles create light.

Later that day, we were all poolside. My sister sunbathed on a lounge chair, sipping an island juice drink with her nose buried in a romance paperback.

My brother grabbed the mini umbrella out of her drink,

ran past me toward the pool. He grabbed his butt holding the umbrella over his head, and yelled, "Look! I'm Mary Poop-ins!"

The splash of the water caught my sister's legs and doused me. My sister was not amused.

"You are so annoying! I swear you were hit with the idiot stick when you were born!"

"It's just water. Live a little, would ya!" he retorted.

I was also less than enamored. "I hate you! I hate the water! Stupid-head!"

My brother taunted. "Come on, Bobby! You have to learn how to swim sometime."

I wanted nothing to do with the water. "No!"

"You're such a baby."

"Quit it! I don't wanna. Jerk-face!"

"Ooooh! Big words for a little man."

"Davey! Leave him alone. The water scares him outta his mind ever since he fell in the William's pool. Can't you give it a rest for five minutes so I can work on my tan in peace?"

"Whatever you wish my queen," he mocked.

As I slid further back from the pool, I looked up and spotted a yellow bird on a palm tree. I pointed my thumb up at it and winked as the sun peeking through the leaves made me squint.

As I brought my gaze back down to the pool's edge, my eyes readjusted to discover a young slender Jamaican man standing before me. The man was dressed in white pants, white slip-on sneakers, no socks, and a white t-shirt with red block letters, "POOL MAN," emblazoned on it. His pant legs were rolled up, exposing his ankles, and his t-shirt was tucked neatly into his pants.

What made him more intriguing to me was the pool skimmer he held commandingly in one of his hands. He looked like Moses ready to part the Red Sea.

"And what might be your name, little man, and where might you be from?"

"I'm Bobby, and I'm from New York," I proudly said. "That's my sister Karen over there. She's really nice." I brought a condemning gaze toward my brother. "...and he's my doofus brother Davey."

"Well, I'm Alex...*The Pool Man*...and you're on my island now." He ran his finger across the letters on his shirt as he said the words, Pool Man. "So what seems to be the problem with you and the water?"

I was evasive. "I can't swim."

"Well, little man. I guess we'll have to do something about that... won't we? This is an important skill you must have. How 'bout you be meetin' me here tomorrow afternoon with your family and I will teach you?"

I was excited. "Can you really teach me?"

His confidence and soulful demeanor spoke to my soul. I knew him. Somehow, I felt like I'd always known him, and he knew me. We were old friends.

"I've taught all the children in my village how to swim, so you can't be too much of a challenge for Alex. After all, I am the Pool Man." He again ran his finger across the letters on his shirt for emphasis.

The next afternoon my mother escorted me to meet Alex. We stood hand-in-hand at the entrance to the pool area. I was holding a G.I. Joe dressed in diving gear in my other hand. I couldn't wait for my mother to meet my friend, Alex. "There he is, Mommy. That's Alex the Pool Man." I was wearing a huge smile.

"So you're the one he's been yabbering about all night long."

"Yes, ma'am! Is it alright that I teach him to swim? He will be a righteous fish when I'm done with him."

My mother fussed through her purse. "Can I pay you for this?"

"No ma'am. The resort pays me plenty. It would be my honor to do this, and it's no trouble at all. No trouble."

"You're too kind. He's really taken with you, ya know."

I positioned my G.I. Joe on one of the lounge chairs near the pool's edge to oversee the operations.

"Okay, little man! Come to Alex here in the pool. I won't let anything bad happen to you. It's time to teach you to be weightless, just like the clouds in the heavens above you. This happens when you're no longer carrying the fear that's holding you down."

I slowly entered the water and made my way to Alex.

I trusted him. We practiced various rudimentary swimming techniques, we splashed each other, and we had fun with the water. He knew what he was doing on many levels. Learning, overcoming fear—it needed to be fun. Laughter defeats the fear in your heart.

"This time, I want you to let go of all your fear. You must go under the water and push your feet off the bottom. You will glide like a bird to me, I promise. Remember to flap your wings like I showed you."

I hesitated for a second, but then was overcome with a peace I hadn't known before. I held my breath, squinched my eyes, and went under the water. When I surfaced, I swam a short distance to Alex's outstretched arms.

"Did I do it?"

"You did it, little man! You did it! Remember what I taught you here today—when you lose your fear, anything becomes possible in life. *Anything!*"

That evening my mother, sister, and I were walking along a dimly-lit paved walkway near the pool area. I was trailing behind them with my beach towel around my neck. As we passed the pool area, I paused, and doubled back to the pool gate. My mother and sister were unaware I'd left the group. The pool area was now closed and devoid of people. I surveyed the chairs and spotted my G.I. Joe who was still stoically watching over the pool yard.

When I ran to retrieve him, I tripped and fell into the pool. For a moment, I had no idea where I was. I was weightless.

I liked the feeling. I surfaced and swam to the pool ladder, just as Alex had taught me.

Moments later, my mother and sister arrived at the pool area. Both had ashen-colored faces when they noticed the open pool gate with my beach towel lying on the ground just inside it.

I could hear my mother's grave voice in the distance. "Oh, my God! Oh, my God!"

As they ran into the pool area, I emerged from the shadows sopping wet from head to toe, holding up my G.I. Joe with a half-smile. "Found him!"

My mother quickly scooped me up into her arms. "Oh, my God! Are you alright? I thought I lost you forever! You're gonna give me a heart attack one of these days. Don't you ever do this to me again."

"Do what Mommy? I was just swimming like Alex the Pool Man showed me."

The following day I was on a quest to see Alex as soon as possible. I couldn't wait to share with him what I'd done. I could swim for real, and Alex gave me this gift. He also saved my life on many levels.

I tugged on the shirt of a resort worker and quizzed him about Alex's whereabouts. "He's off diving down at the beach. He should be just finishing up. You can catch him down there," he said, pointing toward the open beach.

I spotted Alex in the distance emerging from the surf carrying a piece of white coral and a weathered diving mask. I quickly ran to him.

"Alex! Alex! I swam all by myself last night! It was dark and scary, but I did it anyway."

"Whoa...slow down there, little man. What you be doin' in the pool at night?"

"I fell in and swam to the ladder like you showed me. My mommy said you're an angel, and my daddy said you're a hero for teaching me."

He was beaming with enthusiasm. "That's wonderful news, but I'm no hero, and I'm still working on the angel part. Today, we celebrate! I have a special reward for you, my friend. I'm so proud of you."

"A reward?"

"Yes! I will take you to my secret treasure trove of precious shells and beautiful coral—and here's the best part...you can have as much of it as you can carry."

My mind was swimming in the thought. "Really? Treasure!" Visions of pirate treasure chests filled my mind. I was dripping with anticipation.

"You earned it...but you must promise me one thing. You cannot tell anyone where my treasure is, because I sell it to the tourists—to buy food for the children in my village up in the mountains."

"I promise I won't tell! Not even to my brother."

As we walked side-by-side along the beach on the quest to get to his hidden treasure trove, the ocean surf met our feet. I'd occasionally try to walk in his footprints.

"Where do you get all your treasure?"

"The ocean always provides, just like God. I hold my breath for a very long time and dive deep in the ocean. That's where all the best treasure is."

"Do you get scared sometimes?"

"I've had some close calls, but it's worth the risk for the sake of all those who depend on me. I'm always thinking about the children in my village. The Lord provides them with almost everything they need...Alex helps with a little bit with the food when he can." He patted his heart. "When you are lionhearted like me, you face your fears to make something good happen."

"Do I have a lion's heart?"

His teeth glistened in the sunlight as his laughter splashed across them.

"You have the heart of a tiger cub, and it will grow in time."

Suddenly, I saw a purple balloon in the ocean surf, and I made a mad dash for it. "Look a balloon!"

Alex pounced on me like a cheetah chasing its prey. He hooked me under his arm and threw me back onto the beach a second before my outstretched hand reached the balloon. I hit the ground with a thud and the air left my lungs. The purple orb was a Portuguese man-o-war jellyfish. I watched the mass of tentacles wrap around Alex's legs. Alex had positioned himself to protect me. He kicked off the jellyfish, and then ran through the ocean surf to check on me.

He waved his hands above the ground. "That is no balloon!

That's a very bad jellyfish, and it's the biggest one I've ever seen. If it touches you, you will be no more." His tone grew serious. "That creature is filled with burning poison, and we are too far from any doctor to help you if it stings you. You understand this...right?"

As he spoke, I saw newly formed red burn marks begin to appear on his legs. He also had several other scars on his legs I hadn't noticed until this moment.

I cried at the sight of the burns. I thought I'd lose him. "But it got you. Are you going to die? I don't want you to die."

"Don't worry little man. Alex has been diving in these treacherous waters for a long time. I've built up resistance to the sting of those terrible creatures."

I pointed to the scars on his legs. "Did you get all of those diving for treasure?"

Alex rubbed beach sand on the fresh sting marks. "I'm afraid so, but just like the ocean, love knows no depths your heart can't reach. I give thanks to God for all I am able to do for my village, even if I get hurt a bit trying to help them."

I knew what I needed to do. There was a burning desire in my heart. "Can I go to your village? I really want to go there. I want to meet the children."

"We'll see. I've told them all about you, and how special you are. You have a very special soul, little one. I know they'd love to meet you one day. Now let's get you that treasure I promised."

Alex ran into the trees lining the beach. When he returned, he was carrying a bamboo pole. He proceeded to stab the jellyfish and then tossed it into the tree line. "Now that terrible creature won't bother anyone else!"

A short time later, we reached his treasure area. It was a camp-like clearing in the forest area. In the center of the camp, there was a huge tower of shimmering shells surrounded by exotic coral, sea sponges, wooden crates, a makeshift worktable, nets, driftwood, and other objects he'd collected from the ocean.

"Whoa! I can have anything here?"

"Anything you can carry. Come. Come. Look here. I picked out this for your family." He held up a beautiful sculpture-like coral piece. "I had to battle a shark to get this one."

"Really? A shark?"

"Oh, that and more! I also have these little gems for you." He gently placed small pearlescent shells into my hand. He carefully closed my hand over the shells and placed both his hands around them. He knelt next to me. "These are special shells just for you, so you will always remember me and the time we've spent together...even when we don't see each other anymore. You will be my friend always...because you always have been. Know this."

I looked deeply into his eyes and then hugged him. I could see such kindness in him. I realized that our time together in this life would be short. I would soon go home, and I knew I would never see him again. The gifts he gave me were to be a lasting reminder of him, and our time together.

Have you ever really thought about what you are blessed with in your life? A blessing can be anything you're thankful for—your family, your friends, and anything else that contributes to your happiness and wellbeing. This kind gesture was one of those moments. A true friend is someone who celebrates your high points, lifts you out of a low point, and they carry your precious heart through it all. I felt this precious light in Alex.

Later that night, I carefully arranged the various shells and coral Alex had given me on a bed in our cottage. I placed a beach towel over the large coral piece and other precious treasures. I stood proudly in front of the cache as the family waited just outside the door.

"Alright! You can come in now. This is what Alex the Pool Man gave me...cuz I'm a good swimmer."

My brother was the first to scramble in. He picked up a beautiful conch shell and held it up for all to see. "Wow! Are all these for us? Can I have this one?"

"It's part of the treasure Alex sells to get food for the children in his village. He told me he almost dies sometimes when he swims to the bottom of the ocean to get these."

I lifted the towel to reveal a beautiful sculpture-like coral piece, a finely crafted shell necklace, and a Coke bottle filled with small shells.

"These are for you guys from Alex. He said we are all part of his family...the one that lives in his heart always."

I handed the necklace to my sister. She immediately wore and modeled it. I poured some of the shells out of the Coke bottle into my brother's anxiously awaiting hands. The crown jewel was the coral centerpiece for my parents. I couldn't wait to present it to them.

"This is a special one Alex picked out just for you. He had to fight a shark for this."

My mother beamed. "Oh, my. This is even more beautiful than the ones I saw for sale in the gift shop. I'm not sure we can accept this."

I quickly refuted. "Alex said so. This treasure is for us."

This celestial coral piece stayed on display in my parent's house for the rest of their days. Alex left his lasting majestic imprint on our family.

My rally began. I had visions of the village Alex described, and I wanted nothing more in the world than to meet the children there. The quest was set in my heart, and I became a broken record. I drove my parents crazy until they relented.

"I really, really, wanna to go to his village. I wanna see the kids there. Alex can take me there. He said he would. Can I go?"

My mother gave my father her unchallengeable, "You know we need to do this" glance, and she pulled him aside for a hushed discussion.

"John...that man saved him again today. Bobby told me Alex was stung by a poisonous jellyfish that he protected him from. He risked his life for him. Bobby has also been talking non-stop about wanting to visit his village in the mountains. Under normal circumstances, we'd probably never do this...but I know in my heart we should. That Alex is a good man. You know he is."

He relented quietly. "You're right. He's been his guardian angel. I'll talk to him and the resort people tomorrow to see if we can make the arrangements. I can't make any promises, but I'll try. If I can make this work, well...it might be a good learning experience for him."

"...and us," she replied.

My mother was a devout Catholic who rarely missed a week of church. She always had God's big picture in her heart, and she loved to seize a faith-filled teaching moment for us. She knew we were held in God's hands. She knew this was God's work.

Every ounce of love you've discovered is part of an endless heavenly sea that surrounds you at all times. To access it, you just have to open your heart and dip your toes into those precious waves. Spend today discovering just how precious the love in your heart truly is.

FIVE
THE AWAKENING

"I honor the place in you in which the entire
universe dwells. I honor the place in you, which is of
love, of truth, of light and of peace. When you are in
that place in you, and I am in that place in me,
we are one."

— *The Definition of Namasté*

A flower awakens its delicate petals to caress the morning dew, only to dance and rejoice in the precious light of this new day. Isn't it wonderful that you're meant to shine in that very same way? Be open to the unexpected. Rejoice in the majesty of life's little moments and know your greatest wealth resides in your heart. You are meant to share that beautiful treasure.

On the second-to-last day of our vacation, the plan was set for me to visit Alex's village. Alex was simply elated. The glowing smile he wore while he sat behind the wheel of his rusted Ford Fairlane said it all. His car may have seen a better day, but he also had a wonderful one planned for me.

My parents saw me off, and I quickly climbed in the front passenger seat.

"Be respectful of everyone and make sure you use your manners. Okay, honey," my mother said as she kissed my forehead.

Alex smiled and patted my shoulder. "Today is a very special day for you, my friend. Very special. Everyone in my village is prepared for your arrival today."

My imagination was running wild. "Is your village at the tippy top of the mountain...near heaven?"

"We are all the way at the top...as close as we can be to heaven. God's majestic views of the ocean are only ours to behold there." The pictures he painted in my mind only made my eagerness boil over. Alex tapped his hand on the steering wheel with excitement. He was celebrating all the surprises he'd planned for me.

"But first, we must make a stop. I'm havin' a righteous bamboo drum made for you."

This made my enthusiasm explode with nuclear frenzy.

A short time later, we pulled into a large, dirt, open area adjacent to a sawmill. My nose was pressed to the car window while my eyes drank in the strange surroundings. A few young Jamaican men were conversing with each other around a large metal drum. Various stacks of cut bamboo lumber lined the yard. The sounds of a sawmill blade periodically filled the air.

"Alex! Weh yuh up to dis fine day! We almost got dis one tuned man. Have a listen," yelled one of the men from the group. He motioned Alex to join him as another man began playing a homemade kettledrum. "What do you think?"

Alex was pleased. "It's good. It's good, man!"

I was standing next to the open car door, when the man noticed me. "Is that your friend with the angel's soul you keep talkin' about?"

Alex motioned me forward.

"Little man. Come. Come. Come meet my friend, Martin."

Alex stood proudly behind me as he placed his hands on my shoulders. "Martin...meet my friend Bobby. Spirit tells me he has an important mission in this life. He is one of God's righteous messengers, and he will do many good things in this world."

Martin bent down to shake my hand. "Well, big up yourself...a friend of God and my good man, Alex, here is a friend o' mine. I'm honored to meet you, little man!"

Alex turned his attention to the sawmill. "Is it ready, man?"

"Sure thing, man. I cut it first thing dis mornin'. Whatcha be thinkin'? It's right here." Martin held a small handcrafted bamboo ceremonial drum behind his back just out of my view. "I even put some decorations on the side, just like you asked."

"Nice! Nice!"

Martin turned his focus to me. "Now...how 'bout closin' your eyes and puttin' your hands out to receive this righteous gift?"

My hands sprang out in anticipation. As quickly as the drum arrived to them, my eyes popped open. "Whoa!"

"Now it's with its rightful owner," Martin exclaimed. "Let's celebrate this fine little brother."

The group of men cheered and began playing the kettledrum in celebration. I was indoctrinated. I learned that giving was as important as receiving. Every single day is a gift, and I was ready to receive each one with all my heart!

The next leg of our journey brought a winding mountain road with thick vegetation on one side and a beautiful ocean view on the other. I was fixated on the celestial views washing across my window. When we reached the top, we pulled into a large, unpaved clearing. Directly in front of us was a single large avocado tree bearing fruit. The sky was deep blue, and the aquamarine ocean was visible below just beyond the tree. The view was so majestic that I felt like I was in heaven.

Through the windshield, Alex pointed to the avocado tree as the car came to a stop. "That is our tree of life! It bears much fruit to keep my village healthy."

Alex hopped out of the car and took a deep breath of the ocean air and motioned for me to follow. "Come! Come!"

I curiously surveyed the area and found a modest village with dirt pathways throughout. The houses were small single-roomed rustic structures with thatched roofs, dirt floors, and white adobe-like plaster siding. As Alex took my hand, I noticed an elderly Jamaican woman working with a trowel repairing the clay steps of one of the houses. "Why is your grandma making steps? Where I come from, workmen do that."

Alex smiled. "Here in my village, we all help build our

community. Everyone is equal, and we all share equally."

My attention returned to modest surroundings. I saw a young boy emerge from one of the houses with no shoes, wearing dirt-stained shorts and a torn red and white striped shirt. The boy was smiling.

I curiously looked up at Alex. "Are you people, poor people?"

He released a hearty laugh. "We may not have a lot of money here, but our hearts are always rich with love. That's where true happiness comes from."

The air suddenly filled with laughter from a large group of nearby children spilling out of the village. The children were all barefoot and wearing worn tattered clothes. As they approach me, their laughter transformed into singing.

A beautiful traditional Jamaican Christian gospel reggae song flowed into my ears. Each child carried a tropical fruit— bananas, avocados, pineapples, coconuts, mangos, guava, and other island fruit. Alex backed up to allow the group to surround me. They were singing and laughing as each one made eye contact with me. It was overwhelming on so many levels. One by one, they began placing their fruit in a circle around my feet.

I was embarrassed by all the attention, I blurted out, "No— it's okay. You don't have to do this for me—I'm just like you."

They just continued to shower me with fruit and smiles.

As the children began to increase their circle around me, I noticed a few of the boys break from the group to climb the avocado tree.

They motioned for me to raise my hands. One of the boys tossed me a freshly picked avocado. "More for you! More for you! Come! Come!"

The group of children surrounding me then separated a bit to allow access to me for an approaching elderly Jamaican villager. The elder was carrying a crown made from woven palm leaves. When he reached me, he ceremoniously bowed and placed the crown upon my head.

Alex emerged from the village with a donkey in tow. He hoisted me onto the animal and led us on a path toward the houses in the village. "Now you are a righteous prince, my friend."

I was ceremoniously paraded around each of the houses in their village. The children continued to sing while they followed me. After marching around the village, we stopped in front of the large avocado tree. Alex lifted me off the donkey, hoisted me onto his shoulders, and pointed to the shimmering aquamarine ocean below.

"Look down there beyond our tree of life, and you will see all the beauty God has created. There is the treasure, little man. There is the real treasure. Remember this moment," he said with conviction.

This grace-filled moment is the heavenly picture Alex painted for me. It is permanently emblazoned on my heart. Years later, I learned that the ceremony the Jamaican villagers performed for me might be something they do when they welcome a spiritual leader to their village. I felt the magic of this moment. I was awakened—my heart, my soul, and my reverence for others.

The next morning my family solemnly packed their bags and headed out to the curb, awaiting our ride to the airport. I was anxiously scanning the resort ground for Alex when he appeared from behind the flora along the sidewalk. He slowly approached us.

I never wanted to forget Alex. "Mommy, can you take the picture of me and Alex before we go?"

My mother photo-documented just about every moment of our lives, but with all the emotion stirring in our hearts, she almost missed this one. "Oh dear. Where has my mind been? Quick! You two stand over there."

She rummaged through her bag and pulled out her Polaroid camera as Alex and I stood together. He gently placed his hand on my shoulder and cracked a shy smile.

While the photo was developing, Alex knelt next to me, placed his hands on my shoulders, and looked deeply into my eyes. "I will never forget you, little man. Never."

"Will I see you again?" Sadness flowed through my heart.

Alex touched his heart. "Perhaps not in this life...but you will always be right here in my heart...forever."

I hugged him as tears welled up in both of our eyes. "I won't forget you ever."

Dajaun's cab pulled up to the curb, and he hopped out. "And how's my good family doin' on dis fine day?"

I hugged Alex. "I don't wanna go home," I moaned.

My family and Dajaun could only stand vigil over us.

My mother grabbed my father's arm and pointed to the suitcase that was set aside. "Bobby has something for you Alex."

My father stepped forward, holding the suitcase and presented it to Alex. "He's only going home with the clothes on his back and the things you gave him. Last night he begged us to give you all his clothes to take to your village—for the children there. Please take this. It's the very least we can do for all you've done for him."

Tears streamed down Alex's cheeks as he placed his hand on my head.

A huge smile drew across Dajuan's face. "It looks like you might be leaving some things here, but I see dat you're taking something home wit yah that's even more precious....love. Yeah, Man! God is good! God is good!"

This act is the third time Alex saved my life...more, so he saved my soul. He taught me that peace is the whispering stillness spoken by the compassion in every loving heart.

Indeed, you can't run on empty, yet I know that there are people who wake up every day with this sorrowful feeling in their hearts. Sharing a simple smile, saying a kind word, or just one small act of compassion before each day ends is how you walk a divine path. These little gestures may seem meaningless, but they're worth the world to anyone holding emptiness. If you happen to be one of these poor souls, know the angels are right there with you—you're never alone, and divine love will never leave your side.

Six
QUICKSAND

"The sweetest defeat you'll ever have is when
your heart surrenders to divine love."

— Robert Clancy

Was my life spared for a reason—a greater purpose? That question will swim forever in your mind when you've come close to death. In my few years I'd already learned firsthand that someone can be saved by teaching them a lifesaving skill, by risking your life for theirs or by giving them an opportunity to save others.

Alex was my spiritual guide on this subject, and he was a master. My lessons weren't over yet—far from it. Life is a precious gift, and I was about to learn just how fragile and how quickly it could end. When I reflect back upon on all the times I was at death's door, I'm profoundly reminded that it was the hand of God that pulled me away from that dark, cold handle.

Weeks after I returned from Jamaica, I settled comfortably into my regular play routines again. I'd head up to our neighborhood circle to meet my friends and set our plans—

many of which involved playing in the woods behind our neighborhood. We'd spend hours in the swamps catching frogs, building makeshift forts, and trying to avoid the proverbial *wet-foot* during balancing acts crossing the swamps. I can't even begin to count the number of sneakers I ruined back there.

Today was a typical romp in the swamp, like every other normal summer day. I was with a few of the neighborhood boys, Greg, Pat, and Pat's younger brother Tony. We were searching for frogs when we came upon something interesting.

"Guys! Check this out," Greg exclaimed as he poked a stick into a gelatinous mix bubbling up next to the swamp. "It's like Jello."

"More like chocolate pudding," I said.

Without hesitation, Pat jumped onto it, "More like rubber goop. Watch this!"

We all laughed as Pat made funny faces bouncing up and down on the spongy mud trampoline.

"You have to keep jumping, or you sink," Pat said. "Watch." He paused for a moment, and the mud seeped up around his sneakers.

"Lemme go. Come on, Pat! My turn," Tony moaned.

Greg shoved Tony forward. "Alright. Let the snot have a turn before he wets his pants."

"Bobby is next after you, so you better get off quick," Pat commanded. "...and you better keep jumping. If you stop, your feet will be covered with mud, and I'm not spraying them off this time. Your socks smell like a doody diaper." Pat pinched his nose and stuck his tongue out to accentuate his point.

"I can't. I got my new sneaks on. I can't get 'em muddy, or my mom will kill me."

Pat barely got off the mud when Tony jumped onto it. He belly-laughed while he bounced. The fun he was having made me wish I still had my old sneakers, but my mother had tossed them into the trash earlier that week.

"I'm next then," Greg exclaimed. "Okay, Professor Doody Butt. Time's up!"

After Greg finished his round, I placed a rock carefully onto the center of the muddy sludge. "Let's see what else this stuff does." We watched the stone slowly sink onto the chocolate abyss.

Pat grabbed the longest straight branch he could find and shoved it into the slop. It, too, slowly disappeared into the depths of the slurry. "This stuff is like that Blob from outer space, only that one grew and ate the whole city."

"Do you think this goes all the way to China?" Greg asked.

I shrugged. "I dunno. Maybe."

"Hey, it's almost dinner time. I gotta go, or my dad will take his shoe to my butt if Tony and I are late again. I'm responsible for this twerp today." Pat grabbed Tony by the scruff of his collar. "And don't tell anyone about this. This is our secret. I don't want anyone messing this up."

I ran home to be greeted by a traditional Irish family

dinner—corned beef and cabbage. I didn't think much of the dinner or the table conversation that night. My attention was sharply focused on returning to the muddy trampoline. I was more than curious. I was on a mission.

After dinner, I scuttled off to our basement to find my black plastic boots. They were stored somewhere with our winter gear. I tore into the pile of wintery fluff with the intensity of a nor'easter.

As soon as I found them, they were on my feet, and I was on my way back to the chocolate pudding. I was going to get a good long turn of the muddy springboard.

I was alone and made my way back to the secret mud pie.

Thump! Both of my boots touched down on the surface of the chocolate moon. I was elated. I began to jump up and down in pure ecstasy. This came to an abrupt end when one of my boots got stuck. While I was trying to free that foot, the other one became trapped. I quickly began to sink while I struggled to free myself.

After only a few minutes of writhing about in the slurry, the mud poured into my boots, and I sank up to my knees.

My thoughts raced to the trouble I was facing when I got home. My pants were ruined.

"Mommy is gonna be so mad at me!"

I started to panic when the mud reached my thighs. The rising mud made me thrash my upper body about causing the goop to swallow me up even faster.

When the muddy soup reached my waist, I grabbed a small pine sapling with my right hand. It was the only thing I could reach. I knew it wasn't strong enough to pull myself out with, but there was comfort in knowing I had something to hold onto. Feverishly, I tried to dig the mud out from around myself with my left hand. That arm quickly got stuck too. When the muddy monster swallowed up my left arm to my shoulder, I was in sheer terror. I screamed and cried for help as dusk set in.

"Someone please help me! I don't wanna die! Please! Help! Someone help!"

My chin came to rest on the muddy abyss. Only my head and my right forearm remained out. I was still vigilantly holding the pine sapling.

My screams for help fell on deaf ears. I knew I only had minutes left to live. I was physically and emotionally exhausted from my attempts to get free. I lost hope. Sorrowful thoughts engulfed my mind.

"I won't ever be able to tell Mommy and Daddy that I love them. They'll never see me again. I don't wanna hurt them."

Heartbroken, I surrendered. My body fell limp.

They say when you think you are about to die, your life flashes before you. It didn't. I only had images of pure love for all those who cared for me.

Suddenly, a feeling of complete peace cradled me. I stopped crying and struggling, and the tiny pine sapling came into focus. I was at peace with my fate.

Up to this point, I had only thought of this small tree as a tiny comfort. Now that I was eye-to-eye with it, I discovered the beauty in how the needles wrapped the stem. It was God's math. I felt that divine presence in everything around me.

Suddenly a soothing voice spoke to me. I can't say for sure if I heard it with my ears, my mind, my soul, or all three.

"Do one more cry for help. Do it right now. Just one," it commanded.

I hesitated for a second. I'd been screaming my brains out for nearly an hour. No one was coming.

"One more call for help...now," it insisted.

I released a single whimpering cry into the gray dank air.

Minutes later, a large figure appeared at the far end of the swamp. I couldn't believe my eyes. I cried in gratitude. As the tears cleared from my eyes, I saw a man wearing green chest-high waders. His thick beard and red flannel shirt made him reminiscent of Paul Bunyan. I smiled.

"Here! I'm here! Please help me, Mister! Help me!"

At the sound of my voice, he narrowed his focus on my direction. Debris and downed trees in the swamp slowed his pace. He was cracking limbs as he trudged through the muck. Every snap was a glorious symphony in my heart. I was going home—and maybe I'd been there all along.

"Easy there, fella. Let me get my footing, and I'll pull you out. Okay? We don't need both of us stuck in this."

I nodded while his feet straddled the sides of the mud trap, and he hooked me under my arms. It took all his strength to free me. On the third pull, a colossal suction sound broke the silence, and my feet surfaced without my boots.

"Holy moly! You got yourself in there pretty good, didn't you? How on earth?"

My tube socks dangled in the air off my feet like two long brown slimy snakes. The man hoisted me over his shoulder and carried me back through the swamp to his back yard.

The whole time I stared at the trap that nearly killed me until it was out of view. When we entered the man's yard, he set me down on a picnic table bench perched on a concrete patio.

I was shaking uncontrollably, not from being cold, but from the stress. The man's wife quickly wrapped a blanket around me. It took me a moment to realize they were the Kowalski family from our neighborhood. Their oldest daughter Lois was a couple of years younger than I was.

"John just told me you were out there all alone. You poor thing. You must have been so scared. Thank God we let Lois and Kimmy out back to pick up their toys when we did. Lois thought she heard a cat stuck in the woods, and she begged her daddy to save it."

Lois peeked out from behind their sliding glass door. "Mommy, that's Bobby. He's the boy who lives down the street in the gray house."

I'm surprised she recognized me. I was covered from head-to-toe in mud. I must have been quite a sight to see. I don't think I've ever been that dirty since.

"We'll get you home right away, sweetie, okay? I'm sure your mommy and daddy are worried about you." She gently wiped the mud off my face and neck. "You're safe now, honey. It's a miracle John found you. He almost didn't go out there, but Lois kept begged him to find the cat. She only heard the one cry."

John wiped the mud off his hands with a rag and unbuckled his waders. "If he was a cat, he just used up one of his nine lives."

Mrs. Kowalski lined the backseat of their car with towels for me, and her husband drove me home. My father spent about a half-hour using our garden hose to rinse the mud off me while Mr. Kowalski explained to my mother what had happened. Her face was riddled with concern.

While she dried me off, she gently smiled. "Thank the Lord for Mr. Kowalski."

I was just happy to see her face again. I looked lovingly into her eyes. "I love your smile Mommy. Just before the mud ate me up, I heard a voice. It told me to cry one more time, and then Mr. Kowalski came and got me."

She quickly scooped me up. "Oh, God. Oh, dear God in heaven." Her gaze then turned to the sky.

At the following Sunday mass, my mother prayed a bit longer than usual. We both did.

When hope knocks upon your heart, let faith unlock the door and allow divine love to open it to the light of a new day. Your precious soul deserves these heavenly guests. Life's outcomes may not always be what you expect, but they're always what you need at the time, no matter how difficult the challenges you've faced. Trust that there is a higher purpose God has planned for you.

Life becomes crystal clear when you focus your heart on what God intended it for. Whenever you're faced with a difficult question in your life, trust your heart. When you're faced with a difficult question in your heart, trust your faith.

ROBERT CLANCY

SEVEN
THE FINISH LINE

"If you can't fly then run, if you can't run then walk,
if you can't walk then crawl, but whatever you do
you have to keep moving forward."

— *Martin Luther King Jr.*

There are times when a seemingly simple act of compassion or a kind word creates profound endless ripples of love in the universe. A miracle is born in every one of those acts of kindness. It's in every smile you share with another to ease their burdens. The dark mist of despair is dispelled by the glimmering light of one loving heart.

The fall quickly descended upon my neighborhood. Leaves drifted from the maple trees in my yard like brightly-colored tissue paper. A pumpkin and some gourds garnished our front, along with some Indian corn that hung prominently on our front door.

I was jumping in a pile of leaves in my front yard when Mrs. Kellerman, a neighbor from across the street, caught my eye. She was fondly staring at me while I played with the leaves.

She was stylishly dressed in a chic poncho, bellbottom pants, calf-high boots, Jackie-O style sunglasses, and a black felted wool French beret pulled down on her head.

When I stopped jumping for a moment, she motioned for me to come to her. As I approached, she smiled meekly as she took off her sunglasses to reveal a subtle sadness in her eyes.

I beamed a huge smile back at her. "Hi Mrs. Kellerman. Where have you been? Do you wanna race me around the block again today? I gotta a new pair of sneaks!"

She spoke with a light German accent. Her voice was frail. "You're such a sweet boy. I don't know if I'm up for a race today, but how 'bout we powerwalk instead. I don't think I'll be running much anymore. I'm afraid jogging is no longer in my future."

I was excited to know more about this new powerwalking concept. "Sure! What's that?"

Her spirits lifted a bit. "It's where we walk as fast as we can, but we don't run...that would be cheating. My doctor said that's all I can do now...walk. Are you up for the challenge?"

"Sure...but how come you can't run anymore?"

"I'm very, very sick...and I won't be getting better. I only have one lung now."

I gave her a curious look from head to toe. "But you don't look sick."

"I know. It's on the inside of my body. After the doctors took one of my lungs, they told me any kind of exercise is good for me. Since I can't run anymore so, I thought I'd at least get out, you know, for a walk."

I smirked. "Can we still race?"

I grabbed a stick and placed it on the road to create our makeshift finish line. "First one to reach this, wins!"

"Oh, you better watch yourself, Mister, I'm an expert power-walker!"

The race was on. I took my fast-paced walk into a short sprint, then back to a quick step to get the jump on her.

She chased after me the best she could. "Hey! That's cheating!"

I turned around and made a face at her. "I'm still in front of you, ain't I?"

We laughed and egged each other on as we headed off down the block. We circled the block to return to where we had started the race. I was slightly in front of her. I sailed past the finish line with ease and celebrated.

"I win!"

She stopped short of the finish line, bent down to catch her breath, and coughed heavily for a few moments. Her face was ashen. She looked like she'd just finished a marathon race. She straightened up a bit and tried to compose herself, holding a shy smile.

"Are you okay? Mrs. K?"

"Yeah...okay...you got me. You're quite the power-walker Mister."

She made her best attempt to look healthy. "There...I'm all better."

"You don't look so sick. You look okay to me."

Her smile shrank as she paused to reflect. Tear flowed down her cheeks. "I have what they call...*cancer*...and it's very serious...it will make me much sicker very soon. I'm afraid I won't be here when it catches up with me. I'm scared. I'm really scared."

It's the first time in my life I recall hearing the word *cancer*. I was confused about why she looked okay on the outside, yet she was in so much anguish.

"Maybe you can outrun it. Come on! I'll help you. That's what I do when monsters chase me," I said. I held out my hand for her.

She composed herself, lifted her head, and a small smile returned to her face. "You're right...you're absolutely right... let's go!"

We powerwalked together hand-in-hand. I led her around to the finish line. Although she was again winded, she was much more emotionally composed. Suddenly, I jumped behind her so she could cross the finish line first.

"There! You win! Now that *cancer* won't catch up with you."

She dropped to her knees next to me and took me into her arms for a loving hug. Tears were streaming down her cheeks, flowing over the beautiful smile she was holding. "You have no idea what you've done for my soul today...no idea. You are such a precious little boy—you're a guardian angel. You really are."

When the valleys of despair get deep, and the mountains of hope seem too steep, just take each of your steps with faith to conquer those obstacles. You'll find God never lets go of your hand while His angels watch over every one your steps. Whenever fear ends, hope begins.

Let hope become the foundation upon which your strength is built. Let love become your cornerstone where everything in your life begins. Let peace become divine light shining through every window of your beautiful soul. Let faith become your roof, sheltering you from every storm of the heart.

ROBERT CLANCY

EIGHT
A QUIET HERO

*"Great leaders may lead the charge, but quite often
the greatest of those leaders also rescue the hearts
of those in need."*

— *Robert Clancy*

Your circumstances and experiences in life are sometimes the most significant catalysts that define who you are. My father witnessed the worst things one human could do to another during his time in World War II. His introduction to combat was jumping into the ocean off a landing craft on Omaha Beach during the D-Day invasion of Normandy, France.

He was a Private First Class frontline combat medic in the 304 Medical Battalion Infantry. His battalion liberated a concentration camp, and he earned the bronze star for his bravery during a suicidal scouting mission. He rarely talked about the war. When he did, it was typically about his buddy Joe Crowley who watched over him like a big brother.

"Hey, Bobby! I found Pop's war albums. Get down here before Mom catches us." His eyes were lit up like two roman candles. "Hurry! She'll be back home anytime."

I scurried down the stairs to our den. Two leather-bound books were proudly on display in my brother's hands. The albums were filled with black, and white photos held in place with black triangular tabs.

"Look! I found a picture of him with dead Germans all around him."

He opened one of the albums and feverishly flipped through the pages to the photo. "Pop's the one sitting on the bomb, and that's his buddy, Joe, who he talks about sometimes."

"What's he doing with his helmet?"

"He's eating lunch out of it, dummy. They didn't have cooking pots. They used canned rations like baked beans, ham, and stuff, and they cook it up in there. He told me once." His finger then slid over to one of the deceased German soldiers. "Check it out. He's wearing the jackboots like the German G.I. Joe we have."

The soldier was lying on his back, almost as if he was sleeping.

"Do you think Pop killed him?" I questioned softly.

"I dunno. Maybe."

I took the other album and began to absorb the wartime photos. One section contained the pictures of the concentration camp he helped liberate. There were pictures of opened cremation ovens filled with human bones. A skull sat in one of the arched openings bearing silent witness to the horrors that had taken place there. I flipped the page.

"Why did Pop take a picture of this funny-looking tractor in the grass?"

"That's not a tractor. It's an olden-times plow, and that's not grass—it's wheeee—"

As the wheat field wrapping around the tractor came into focus, suddenly he realized it was stacks of lifeless bodies piled ten high for as far as the eye could see. The plow was perched at the edge of a long trench. The sides of the massive grave were powdered with lye. The abandoned plow still had a stack of bodies in its blade.

"Those sick bastards! That wheat field is dead people. Look!"

We were both now fixated on this photo album. The next page of his album was just as horrific as the last. At first glance, we thought we were looking at skeletons in gray striped prison clothes. The group of nearly starved to death victims of the camp had their hopeless hands outstretched through the fence that contained them. Their eyes were empty, soulless orbs.

"Why would someone do this to people, Davey?"

"I dunno. They're really messed up in the head or something." He pointed to my father's framed medals. "You see that bronze star medal? Pop probably got that one for saving these people."

I was proud of him. We both were, but our moment of honor ended abruptly with the shrill of my mother's voice.

"David Patrick Clancy, you better not let me get my hands on you! I told you to stay out of those albums!"

Her feet came to the rest at the top of the stairs. We eyed her hand slipping off one of her shoes.

"I'm gonna tan your backsides for this!"

Although she never hit us, she had a way with words that would scare the living daylights out of us. Her shoe prop weapon added the exclamation point to her threats. We ran for our lives.

"Come on, Bobby!"

"And you're lucky I'm not gonna tell your father about this," she yelled as we ran out the back door. "The good Lord knows he doesn't want to think about those times!"

It was the only time I saw those war photos, but they are burned forever into my mind. My mother sanitized the photo albums and hid them from us.

The following week, my father was out in our back yard, doing some yard work. He spent most summer days without a shirt on, and a cold beer in his hands. My mother was convinced he worshiped the sun.

My brother and I were on our back porch playing with our G.I. Joes. Our mock battle was momentarily disrupted when my father stopped in to get out of the sweltering heat. The sweaty sheen on his chest and arms accentuated the wartime wounds on his skin.

"Is that a scar from the war?" my brother asked.

"Did you get shot there?" I piped in.

"I got 'em in the war, alright, but I wasn't shot. I took some shrapnel in my shoulder and arm from a mortar shell that hit near the truck I was hiding under."

It was apparent he wasn't comfortable with our topic. He glanced at our G.I. Joes. "Luckily, my buddy, Joe Crowley, yelled for me to get out from under that damn truck. The very next round blew the hell out of it."

He chuckled for a moment, and his story took a lighter turn. "Then I ran into a blown-out building scared outta my wits. I tried to get down the stairs to the basement before the next mortar strike when a baby carriage got hooked onto my canteen. All the guys were watching me from the other side of the street."

He wiped another swatch of sweat from his head and smiled. "And there was ol' Joe Crowley again to break the tension of the damn moment. He yells out, 'Look, there goes Clancy with the whole damn family hooked to his ass.'"

We all burst out laughing. It's one of the few times we ever got a war story out of him. The first time he seemed happy about it.

"It's quite a thing to be scared out of your mind and laughing just as much at the same time. Joe always made me feel like I'd make it through, and I did. Thank God. Those were tough times. I was on the Siegfried Line in the Battle of the Bulge, and those krauts weren't giving up. They were Hitler's last line of defense—his most hardened soldiers. We just fought harder."

We wanted more, and my brother hit him with the question.

"Hey, Pop. Did you ever shoot anyone?"

There was dead silence.

Before my brother could retract his words, my father's gaze narrowed in a way I'd never seen before. We both knew we were now in uncharted dangerous territory, and the air in the room darkened. He was angry, but he wasn't mad at us. He gritted his teeth.

"What the hell do you think? It was war! If I didn't go, who else would stand up for those people? Who? I did what I had to do, and that's enough," he yelled. His fists were clenched.

He took a hardened stance and puffed his chest out. "Don't you ever ask me that again! You hear me?"

We never did.

My brother and I looked at the ground. We wanted to disappear into the floor. Slowly our eyes met my father's face again. He was beet red. He gave us one last contemplative glare before he stormed off. He just stood in the back yard, closed his eyes, and allowed the sun to fall upon him.

Just before dinner that night when he knelt next to me. "I'm sorry about earlier. It's not you. I...I had to do things...things we all had to do to save people. It was war times."

He was shaken, but he held his emotional footing like he always did. "I want you to know something. You can be a leader, or you can be a follower. Just know in life anyone can be a good follower, but a good leader is rare. I've seen with my own eyes what bad leaders can do to others. You need to be one of those decent leaders who takes people to a place worth going."

I looked up into his eyes and crossed my heart. "I will, Pop. I promise."

Great leaders may be found at the top of a mountain looking back upon their challenges, but the greatest leaders are often found at the foot of the mountain, still helping others reach that summit. My father was one of those leaders in his own quiet way. He served, and he sacrificed are part of his soul for the betterment of our world. I've always been proud of the leadership he gave to my heart.

My father taught me that there are many roads to take in life, some you choose, and some you have to take, but ultimately, only one ever leads you home.

NINE
PITCHFORKS AND HALOS

"Before you hand down the verdict on someone you've prejudged, confer with love's jury first."

— *Robert Clancy*

When you prejudge people within the shadows of your heart, you may never get the chance to see the pure light radiating from their souls. Before you consider handing down the verdict on someone you've cast aside with your innate prejudice, confer with love's jury first, for the only guilt that's found is buried in your own heart.

It was the spring of 1972, and my elementary school playground was filled with the chatter and laughter of children. A game of kickball would engulf the parking lot nearly every day.

During our recess, Mr. B., a short, stocky, clean-cut gym teacher, would take his familiar stance in the middle of the mix. His face was accented by black-rimmed eyeglasses that matched his equally dark, slicked hair. You would often see him holding a clipboard, with a pencil adorning his ear and a silver whistle attached to a chain jangling around his neck. We all loved him. He was always smiling, and you could tell that he loved being out there with all of us.

In contrast to Mr. B., there was an ominous character at our school who scared the bejesus out of us. He was a tall, lanky, dark-haired emotionless man who looked like actor Fred Gwynne. He was always wearing a gray jumpsuit with a large keychain swinging from his pocket. Husky scuffed black boots adorned his feet. The heel of one of his shoes was much thicker than the other. A metal brace wrapped one of his legs, and he walked with a limp.

Anytime he'd appear in the doorway of the gym to survey the playground, children would scream and scurry away at the sight of him.

During the week before our Easter vacation break, Mr. B. watched fear-stricken kids run past him, and he waved the janitor off.

"Jesus, Jim…you're scaring the hell out of 'em again. Wait 'till recess ends before you start sweepin' up."

Jim mumbled and backed away into the building, disappearing into the shadows. Mr. B. blew his whistle, and we lined up single file.

"Alright. Get your butts back in the building. Fun time is over. Chop, chop, people!"

That day I couldn't wait for the school bell to ring. Easter vacation was only one day away. The bell rang out, and we all spilled out onto the sidewalks like ants exiting a mound. I would always join my awaiting friends, Jeff, Dylan, and Ron. We'd skip past the buses lined up in front of the building like long a yellow passenger train. We all lived close enough to the school to be able to walk home.

My friend, Jeff, was a very tall, skinny blond-haired boy. We met in the second grade and became instant friends. Dylan was the joker of the group, and he just took life as it came at him. Ron and I met when we were just two years old. We'd all spend hours at each other's houses. We were life-long friends, and we never questioned our friendship. It just was.

Jeff was the first to jumpstart that day's conversation. "I was able to do a headstand last night."

"Really? How?" Dylan questioned as he kicked one of the bus tires.

"I laid on the floor and pushed my feet up on the wall. It was easier than I thought it would be."

I was in. "I gotta try that."

Jeff cautioned. "Yeah, well...I was doing pretty good until my mom caught me. I left my footprints all over the wall. She was so mad she used my full name when she yelled at me." He mimicked his mother. "Jeffery Wayne Krauss, do you know what it costs to maintain this household?"

"Holy moly! If I did that, I'd get my hide tanned for sure," Dylan said.

I always seized a moment to rib Dylan. "Don't you mean you'd get a red hiney, like a baboon's butt?"

Dylan's response was always swift. "You mean like when it

gets red like this?" He flicked my ear, and it was burning.

"Quit it, butt-munch! You are such a doof Dylan! I hate it when you do that!"

"Whatever."

Jeff was our great diversionary. "What are you guys doing for the Easter break? Wanna come over to my house?"

"Surrrrrrre......." I stopped in my tracks as I spotted Jim, the janitor, standing on the path dead ahead of us. That day, he looked particularly Frankenstein-esque.

As my eyes grew big, and I held Jeff, Dylan, and Ron back with my arm to protect them. Jim was blankly staring at us. His ominous black jalopy was parked next to the sidewalk with the driver's door wide open. It looked like a hearse awaiting a funeral casket.

We screamed. "Ahhhhhhhhhhhh!!! Run! It's Herman Munster!!!"

We took off running and hid behind the school building. Jim shook his head and got into his car. We watched and waited until the sinister-looking sedan pulled away and exited the parking lot.

I waved us out of hiding. "It's safe now. Come on!"

The next day the school day flowed like any other. Thoughts of my chocolate and jellybean-filled basket dominated my thoughts.

Mrs. Kruczkowski meandered to the head of the class. She was wearing a beaded chain around her neck that was attached to the tortoiseshell cat eyeglass frames adorning her face. She had a slight Polish accent and looked like Dr. Ruth Westheimer.

In her classroom, various art projects decorated the walls. Wooden painting easels encrusted with years of paint lined the outer edges of the room. Boxes of craft materials were stacked on the countertops that lined the windows. We were all fidgeting in our seats, awaiting the class to begin.

I leaned over to Jeff, who was sitting in the desk adjacent to me. I covered my mouth with my hand so the teacher couldn't see what I was saying. We were convinced she could read our lips and our minds. It was hard to get away with any mischief in that class.

"I hope we're makin' something cool today." I stuck my finger in my mouth and acted like I was barfing. "Remember back on Valentine's Day when she had us making heart-shaped ballerinas?"

Jeff snickered as Mrs. Kruczkowski grabbed command. "Hello, my lovelies. I have an Easter art project prepared for you that's near and dear to my heart." She covered her heart with her hands and fluttered her eyelids.

This gesture only made me cringe. I knew what was coming.

"You're all going to make precious little angels that we'll string together to decorate our hallway."

She reached behind her desk and proudly held up a handcrafted angel hanging from a piece of white string. The body of the angel was a Dixie Cup with a robe that was made from layered white and light blue tissue paper. Wings jutted from each side, cut from silver construction paper that was glued to the back of a styrofoam ball. A gold pipe cleaner for the halo completed the look.

"Aren't they simply divine?" she asked.

I groaned and made a disgusting facial expression at Jeff. "This is for girls. It's just dumb. I'm not doin' it."

The rest of the boys followed in unison. "Not again."

The girls swooned with approval of the angelic bliss they'd soon be crafting.

"Okay, children. Line up and get your celestial supplies. Everyone must participate—this includes you boys," Mrs. Kruczkowski said as she set out bins containing the craft materials and supplies. "Line up, people!"

She began handing out the Dixie Cups to each of us.

I sported a mischievous look on my face and turned to Jeff and Dylan, who was directly behind me in line. "I'll show her! I'm makin' a devil," I whispered.

Dylan snickered.

Knowing this was no easy feat in this class, Jeff wanted the plan. "How you gonna do that?"

I was smug. "My dad says, 'Where there's a will... there's a way.' Which drawer does she keep the Halloween stuff in? I just need some black and red paper and a black pipe cleaner."

Jeff gave me a low-five tap on my hand. "Yeah! Do it!"

Each student was busily assembling an angel. Mrs. Kruczkowski was gleefully smiling as she walked down the row desks gazing admirably at all the precious creations, that is, until she reached my desk.

"Do you really think you should be making *that*, Mr. Clancy?"

I smirked. "Well...after all...you can't really have angels without having a devil or two in the mix...right, Mrs. K.?"

I gave a mischievous glance back to Jeff and Dylan and doled out another smug smile to Mrs. Kruczkowski. I proudly displayed my pitchfork-toting satanic masterpiece for all to see. The class giggled in unison at the spectacle.

She was less than enamored. "Well then...I guess I stand corrected, Mr. Clancy...just know that God eventually corrects everything."

Mrs. Kruczkowski peered down at me with a smug grin before she returned to walking down the row of desks, praising those who completed their divine creations.

By the end of the school day, a long string of angels hung along the corridor wall high above the cubbies. The celestial line-up was broken up by a single red and black pitchfork-toting effigy. My devil hung right in the middle of the heavenly mix.

The end-of-day school bell rang out, and I bounced out of my desk. "Yay! That's it! Easter vacation!"

I grabbed my bookbag and ran out of the classroom to meet Jeff and Dylan in the hallway. When our trio passed the spot where the devil hung, Jeff bumped me and snickered as he pointed it out. "You sure showed her."

I proudly smiled as we continued down the hallway. "I hope I get a ton of red jellybeans in my Easter basket this year. They're my favorite!"

Dinner came quickly that day. My father, mother, and brother sat at our usual spot around the kitchen table. My father was wearing his gray industrial work shirt with his General Electric work I.D. badge clipped to the front pocket.

He picked up the beer can that sat next to his dinner plate and took a good swig. "This third shift is killing me Margie...and it's just like that Joe Crowley to call in sick again on a holiday weekend...every damn time!" He shook his head in disapproval and dropped his fist onto the table. The force made all the dinner plates rattle. "And where the hell is Karen tonight?"

"John...the kids...and it's a holy weekend," my mother scolded. "Karen is at her boyfriend's house for dinner. Remember?" She glared at him and flashed three fingers. "And I expect you to say three Hail Marys for that while you're at work tonight...Three!" She then bowed her head and made the sign of the cross.

My brother had a single focus...dinner. "I'm not sure about the three Hail Marys, but I'll take three more slices of that meatloaf."

My mother suddenly pulled the plate of meat away from him. "Oh my God... we're all gonna burn in hell. It's Good Friday!"

"So?" my brother retorted.

She was flustered. "No meat! I must be losing my mind with

you kids."

That didn't stop my brother. Not much could come between him and a slab of meat. He pulled the plate back down to his face and grabbed a slice with his bare hand. "Well... it's a bit late for that now. If I'm goin' to hell, it's gonna be on a full stomach."

He quickly necked down the slice of meat before she could snatch it away from him.

I smirked at my brother and pointed to the floor. "I guess I'm not goin' to hell...I hate meatloaf, and I didn't eat any of it. Ha ha! Say hello to the devil for me, Davey."

"Watch your tongue, Mister!"

"Sorry, Mommy."

I stuck my tongue out at my brother without anyone else seeing me. He returned a death glare.

My mother scowled at my father and shook her finger at him. "They get this from you, ya know."

My father could always ease any tensions with his wit. He shrugged her off while he squinted one of his eyes and mustered up his best Popeye the Sailor impersonation. "I gotta be me...and I yam what I yam! Strong to the finish, cuz I eats my spinach." He forked a clump of spinach from his plate, held it up to her and popped it into his mouth.

"Good one, Pops!" my brother exclaimed.

My father always picked a comeback line from his usual list. "I'll pop ya, alright!" He waved his fist like Popeye would do.

"Are ya still hungry, Davey? How 'bout you go look in the mirror and get fed up!"

I snickered and pointed at my brother as he slumped back in his chair like a defeated boxer.

"I seriously don't know how I survive in this household."

I hastily finished the last bit of my dinner and pushed my plate away. "Mommy, I'm finished. May I please be excused to go play up in my room?"

"Sure, dear."

My mother dished out one more scolding look to my father and brother. "At least someone in this house still has his manners."

I always looked for a way to seize love from my mother and use it to taunt my brother. I strolled past my brother, made a face at him, and then made a mad break for the stairs. He attempted to charley horse my arm but missed his opportunity.

My mother called after me. I could tell by the tone of her voice I succeeded. "Hey, sweetie... don't forget I made some chocolate pudding...your favorite... it's still warm."

"Thank you, Mommy. I'll be down in a couple of minutes. I love you!"

"At least there's still something heavenly in this house," she swooned.

"I swear he gets away with murder," my brother muttered.

I popped into my room and stopped briefly to give a proud nod to a framed photo of President John F. Kennedy that hung next to an Immaculate Virgin Mary holy water font wall sculpture. She was depicted from the waist up with her hands touching a heart on her chest. Light rays radiated from her heart. A tear on her cheek under one of her eyes completed her merciful gaze.

I grabbed my G.I. Joe and posed in a headstand position against my bedroom wall. I studied the G.I. Joe for a moment before saluting him. "Okay...we got this, soldier."

I laid on the floor and began pushing my legs up the wall in an attempt to do a headstand. After a couple of tries, I managed to get into a headstand position. As I pushed myself up a bit higher, I was unaware that my foot lifted the Virgin Mary sculpture off of its perch.

Suddenly the relic fell off the nail. Crack! It smacked me directly on my chin, splitting it open. Blood immediately began to pour profusely from the gash and onto my neck. I fell over onto the floor, groaning in agony.

I was stunned for a few seconds, squinching my eyes as I writhed on the floor. The sculpture weighed about two to three pounds, and I literally saw blue and white stars when the thing hit me.

Blood was now oozing out from between my fingers. As I slowly opened my eyes, they met by the melancholy eyes of the Virgin Mary. She was looking straight at me.

I got myself back to my feet and momentarily looked at her now-scolding glare while I attempted to quell the blood running down my chin.

Tears streamed down my cheeks.

I ran across to our upstairs bathroom and jammed a pile of tissues on the gash. While I held the wad to my chin, I rifled through the medicine cabinet, grabbed a box of Band-Aids, some gauze, and did a simple triage on myself.

My mind turned to the devil I'd made. I didn't want my family to know what I did. This indiscretion was between God and me.

I tried to slip unnoticed past the kitchen doorway. My mother caught a glimpse of me. "Honey...your pudding."

I fibbed to cover up my awful truth. "Uhhh...I left my bike at Jeff's house. I wanna get it before it gets dark out...okay?"

"Don't be too long or it will get cold."

"Okay, Mommy."

I slithered down the back stairs to our den, holding a wad of crimson-stained tissues to my chin. I hastily gathered tape, paper, scissors and a box of crayons from a desk, and then ducked into our basement. I hunkered down at the basement workbench. With my makeshift supplies, I did my best to create an angel with paper, tape, and whatever else I could find down there.

I struggled to hold back my tears and periodically wiping my eyes with my sleeve. When the angel was finished, I looked up toward the ceiling and clasped my hands together to pray. "Please God. Please. I'm sorry I was bad today. Just let me in the school, and I'll put my angel up...I swear I'll be good from now on."

I quickly ran out the back door and frantically pedaled my bike back to the school. The parking lot was completely empty, with the exception of one car. Jim's the janitor's black sedan was parked at the far end. I shuddered.

I hastily dropped my bike on the school sidewalk and ran toward the main school entrance. I pulled several times on the doors, but they were all locked.

My only chance was the side entrance. I repeatedly pulled on the door handle, but it was futile. I'd been defeated. I looked through the glass door where I could see the devil just out of my reach. Centered in the hallway was a large broom leaning against a gray garbage can, along with freshly swept up piles of papers and debris.

I emotionally broke down into the fetal position sobbing at the base of door. "Please let me in. Please let me in. Please God... please...I promise...I'll be good from now on...I promise... I promise...I'll..."

The angel rolled out of my hand onto the ground as I went limp.

Jim must have heard my commotion and started down the hallway toward the door. He rummaged through a huge pile of keys attached by a chain to his jumpsuit pocket. The door unlocked and swung open, and he was standing over me.

"What's the problem, young man?" He eyed the blood on my chin and my discarded bike. "Did you hurt yourself? Jim's here now. It's gonna be okay."

There was such a calm gentleness in his voice. When I looked up, I saw only a tall shadowy backlit figure standing above me. As his face came into focus, his gentle smile appeared.

I was pretty much incoherent at this point. My voice was weak from crying, and I now had the dry cries where you periodically gasp for air in between words. "I have to get in the school...I was bad...I made...a devil...God's mad at me...I have to put my angel up...I don't wanna burn in hell..."

Jim let out a hearty laugh. "Is that all?" He reached out his hand to help me up. "I think I can help fix that. I fix almost everything in this ol' building. How 'bout you show me where that little devil is, and big Jim will take care of that right quick."

I wiped my tears away with my sleeve while I walked down the hallway holding Jim's hand. As we walked side-by-side, I stayed fixed on his face. This was the first time I got a good look at him up close. There was a soulful kindness etched upon him. When we stop halfway down the hallway, I pointed out the satanic effigy to him. "He's right there."

He chuckled. "I was wonderin' who made that."

Jim hoisted me up so I could pull the devil down with my own hands.

"It's your job to take care of that. I learned long ago that your life is always in your hands...and God's. He holds us all in His hands, just like I'm holdin' you right now," he said.

I handed the devil to him and hung my makeshift angel in the newly opened spot.

Jim slid the gray garbage can over to me. "There...that wasn't so hard, was it. How 'bout you put that one where he belongs."

I succinctly threw it away.

"I bet that feels a bit better...huh!"

I nodded. The weight was lifted off my chest, and it felt beautiful. After Jim escorted me back outside, we ended up sitting side-by-side together on the steps of the school.

He extended his hand for a shake. "My name's Jim...and, who might you be little fella?"

"I'm Bobby."

"Well, now that we're properly introduced." Suddenly, he caught me looking at his leg brace. "Oh, that thing." He patted it. "Polio. Got it when I was just a little guy like you. Had it all my life. For a long time, I thought God was mad at me, too."

He glanced at the ground to reflect for a moment then brought his gaze back to my face. "I know I look scary to you kids...but I don't mind so much." He straightened up his bum leg, and a smile slowly drew across his face. "But you see, I've got one of the best jobs in the world. If it wasn't for this bad leg God gave me, I wouldn't have this job where I get to see you little angels nearly every day of life. You see, I'm always thinkin' about your smiles...even when I am sweeping the halls here, I go home counting my blessings every single night." He patted his leg again. "Yeah, I'm blessed."

That moment changed me. I was blessed too. Blessed to have been given the opportunity to stop judging others.

After the Easter break, Mr. B. took his familiar stance in the middle of the playground mayhem holding his clipboard with the same pencil stuck behind his ear. The silver metal whistle around his neck glistened in the sunlight.

Jim, wearing his ever-familiar gray jumpsuit, appeared from the shadows in the gym doorway. As the sunlight slowly illuminated his face, the children noticed him. "Aaaaaaaaaaah! It's Frankenstein, the monster!"

They scattered in all directions, screaming—everyone except me. I cracked a big smile and waved hello to him. He beamed a huge smile back at me from the doorway before he faded back into the shadows.

Never underestimate the great tool you carry with you everywhere...your beautiful smile. It can touch the heart of an old friend, bring radiance to a stranger and most importantly, it can change your whole outlook on life when you share it with yourself.

Love never discriminates. Love doesn't judge. Love just accepts.

TEN
TRUE BEAUTY

*"True beauty is not measured by the love growing
in your heart, but rather by the love you've planted
within the hearts of others."*

— *Robert Clancy*

Asking how to forgive is like asking, "What does God look like?" That image only resides on the blueprints of love written in your heart. What if you could only see that beauty within everyone? What if you saw just the true essence of their souls, and it turned out to be pure love. I always wondered if this is how God and His angels see each of us? I was about to get as close to that answer as humanly possible.

It was evening in the late fall of 1975, and the air of upstate New York was brisk. All of the neighborhood kids were gathered under the Blakes' streetlamp. I was ten years old, and my brother had just turned fifteen.

Two of the Blake girls, Margot, the younger one, along with her seventeen-year-old sister, Sarah, opened the garage door of their house. As the door slid up, the overhead light shimmered across a substantial red kite hanging on the back wall. My

111

brother, Dave, motioned for them to join us.

Dave cupped his hands into a mini megaphone. "Olly olly home come free! Come on in, guys! We're gonna start a new game. Margot and Sarah are playin' this time."

The sisters joined the group under the streetlight. Sarah, one of the prettier girls in the neighborhood, was a slender figure accentuated by long, flowing, straight hair. Margot, the shorter of the two, had bobbed hair, and a tomboyish demeanor. As the girls met up with my brother, a few more kids emerged from the shadows to join.

I was the last to join. "Not fair! I had the best hiding spot that time. You would have never found me."

Dave gave me a push. "I don't have to find you now, punk, and since I just tagged you, you're it this time."

"You stink!"

"Too bad! Loser!"

Margot was always easy-going and immediately quelled our feud. "It's okay. I'll be 'it' for this round. I can never find a good hiding spot anyway."

I was fixated on the kite. "When are you guys gonna fly that thing?"

"Dustin says he's waiting for the perfect windy day. He'll eventually have to get his butt out here with it," Sarah replied.

Margot refuted her immediately. She knew her brother like the back of her hand. "Yeah...right. I think he's just scared he'll lose it in the trees. Dad and him spent weeks working on that thing. You'd think he'd at least test it out or something."

Margot hopped forward and clapped her hands on her thighs. "So...what's the game plan?

My brother laid down the rules. "You give everyone a count to a hundred. No one is allowed past the Okonski's house on this side or the Kellerman's house on that side."

When Margot glanced toward the Kellerman's house, she pursed her lips. "I can't believe Mrs. Kellerman passed away. I don't even know what to say to Danny. I saw him with his dad in their driveway the other day. I just looked down."

My brother was solemn. "Yeah. I know what you mean. It hasn't been the same over there. I avoid goin' past their house when I can."

"I really miss Mrs. Kellerman...and what about Mr. Corbin... what happened to him," I quizzed.

Margot gave my brother a nod of concern as she glanced at me. She leaned into him to try to prevent me from hearing their conversation.

"You didn't tell him about the suicide, did you?" she asked in a hushed tone.

"No. God no! I just told him he was sick. He was one of the last ones to see Corbin alive before he went and did the deed at that hotel."

Margot consoled me. "Mr. Corbin wasn't feeling well...and he...uh... he's with the angels now...you know...in heaven."

Dave reeled us in. "We need something good to happen in

this neighborhood for a change," he said in a definitive tone.

"Our sister Dayna's gettin' married next weekend. Does that count? Weddings always bring love into the air," Sarah said as she shot Dave a demure flirty gaze. Margot glared at her sister when she weaved her arm around his.

"David is my protector. He'll make sure love doesn't get us."

Sarah rolled her eyes.

At this point, I was flustered. "Can we just get the game started already?"

Margot closed her eyes and covered them with her hands as we all scattered into the darkness. "1...2...3..."

***

The following week my mother was busy in her makeshift basement beauty salon. Two bubble hairdryer units were parked against the light wood paneled walls. Mrs. Blake was in the salon chair facing the mirror.

Easy-listening pop music from the '70s emanated from the radio. *"Lovin' you is easy 'cause you're beautiful..."*

I skipped down the basement steps as my mother lifted the top of the Barbicide jar and grabbed one of the combs that popped up. She shook the liquid off the comb, then gave the salon chair a couple of pumps with her foot. After sharing a quick smile with me, she returned to working on Mrs. Blake's hair.

My mother's salon accommodated many of the neighborhood women. Ladies were at our house regularly getting their hairdos done up. I didn't pay much attention to Mrs. Blake that day. I was on a mission to get my new Kung Fu Grip Adventure Team G.I. Joe and the G.I. Joe foot locker stuffed with gear.

"Ahhh, I just love this song," Mrs. Blake announced.

My mother was focused on the task at hand. "You're gonna look gorgeous at Dayna's wedding tomorrow. What time is your rehearsal dinner tonight?"

"It starts at seven o'clock sharp. Boy, oh boy, do I still have lots to do." Her smile widened. "And that's why I come to you, Maggie. You always make me look good...but even better...you make me feel good about myself...and you always fit me in at the last minute to boot. You're a gem."

"Awww. I just love the company and catching up with you."

Mrs. Blake lit up with anticipation. "My oldest daughter heading down the aisle...it just gives me goosebumps!"

"I know what you mean...even Bobby is shooting up. Just look at how tall he is now," my mother exclaimed. She spun the salon chair around so Mrs. Blake could see herself in the mirror. "All done! What do you think?"

Mrs. Blake beamed. "Maggie! I don't know what I would do without you. How much do I owe you?"

"What? Your smile isn't enough?" My mother waved her finger at Mrs. Blake as she removed the plastic haircutting cape. "And don't you kibitz with me over the money. This is my treat."

Mrs. Blake hopped off the chair to hug my mother. "You're

a precious soul and a wonderful neighbor." As she did, she eyed the clock. "Oh, boy...look at the time. I've gotta get back to my house, or they'll start wondering what happened to me."

As Mrs. Blake passed me, she said, "You've got a good mom there... You're ten years old now, right?"

"Yep! I turned ten back in April...so I'm ten and three quarters now," I said, straightening myself up.

She grabbed her fall coat off the wall hook, buttoned it up, and started up the basement steps shaking her head. "Oh, boy. You kids really are growing up way too fast. Where does the time go? Can you do me a favor and walk me out?"

"Sure thing, Mrs. B."

She smiled. "You're such a kind boy. You really are."

I watched her walk down to the end of my driveway before looking away. There was such happiness in her steps that I couldn't resist taking it in. It painted a smile on my face. I headed back to the house to play with my G.I. Joe.

The very next morning, I was abruptly shaken awake by my brother. "Bobby! Get up! Get up!" His face was ominous. "There was a horrible accident last night...it happened on the way back from the wedding rehearsal...their station wagon was rear-ended by some drunk driver...it exploded."

I tried to clear the sandman out of my eyes. "What exploded?"

"Margot, Sarah, Bryant...Mr. and Mrs. Blake," he exclaimed.

I was jolted into consciousness. "Are they okay?"

"All I know is Mrs. Blake didn't make it. They were all burned in the accident. It sounded bad...really bad."

I tried to make sense. "But I saw Mrs. Blake yesterday...she was happy."

"I know. I know. Gas poured in on them. There wasn't anything they could do. Dayna and her fiancé were in a different car...and they saw the whole thing."

"What about Dayna's wedding?"

"There's no way that's happening now...not for a while anyway." He clenched his fists. "I wish I could get my hands on the guy who did this. Just give me five minutes with him. That's all I'll need."

"What can we do? I wanna help them."

"The only thing you can do...pray for them."

I buried myself into my pillow with tears welling up in my eyes. My mind was swimming with images of how happy Mrs. Blake was. How could she be gone? I struggled to search my mind for every kind word I ever said to her. Did I ever even tell her loved her? I wanted her to know. I prayed she did.

The sky was as gray and dreary as the fog of grief that cloaked my neighborhood. David and I join a small group of the kids gathered in the street. We were all lost. Two of the girls hugged each other while tears streamed down their cheeks.

David just angrily shook his head. "I think they're taking Sarah and Margot to the intensive care burn center upstate. It's gonna be months before they'll be home. All because of one worthless dirtbag."

"Is it true Sarah has fifth-degree burns on her face, and Margot and her dad were burned bad too," asked one of the boys.

"I dunno. I think they're taking Sarah and Margot to the intensive care burn center upstate."

One of the girls in the group wiped the tears from her eyes. "Are they in comas?"

Dave gave me that look my father had on his face when we asked him about World War II. "Not sure. All I know is the guy who did this should burn in hell forever."

❦

A couple of months later, I was sitting at our kitchen table eagerly awaiting a grilled cheese sandwich my mother was preparing for me.

"Mommy, where do people go when they die?"

She pushed a spatula down firmly on the bread in the frying pan. "What makes you ask that, Sweetie?"

"Davey said there's a special place in hell for worthless dirtbag losers...like the guy who smashed the Blake's car."

"Sweetie...I don't want you using those words, okay? I think your brother is due to have his mouth washed out with soap."

I pushed further. "Do you think Mrs. Blake is in heaven?"

"Of course, Sweetie. She was practically a saint."

I had to know more. I couldn't understand why God would

allow such a good person to die. "Why did God take her then?"

Her faith was unshakable. She taught me that even the most horrific things were part of God's good plan. "There are a lot of things that happen in this world that don't make sense...at least to us." She pointed toward the ceiling. "They just make sense to Him...and I trust that it's for the better in some way."

She gave a faith-filled nod at the ceiling and slipped the sandwich onto my plate. "I just trust God always knows what He's doing."

David suddenly burst into the kitchen and grabbed half of my sandwich, dabbed it in some ketchup and took a bite. "I heard Margot is coming home from the hospital today. I'm gonna wait for her in the driveway. Come on, Bobby."

He bolted out of the kitchen as fast as he made his entrance.

"That's wonderful news...and for crying out loud, will ya stop teaching Bobby with your foul mouth."

"Oh crap! Sorry, Ma."

She shook her head in disapproval. "Tsk, tsk, tsk! That kid is gonna put me in an early grave," my mother muttered.

When we reached the top of the driveway, we froze in our tracks as Margot slowly walked toward us. Her head was partially bandaged. Scars from burns and a tracheotomy protruded from her jacket. She smiled and waved at us.

We both screamed in excitement. "Margot!"

"I missed you guys so much. I'm so happy to finally be back home."

"How are you feeling? When do your bandages come off?" My brother questioned in rapid-fire.

She just sighed. "Oh, I'm doin' fine, and the bandages will be off soon..." She laughed. "I just don't think my hair will ever be the same again."

My brother smirked and pulled her in for a hug. "You're too funny, but I was serious."

"How's Sarah? Will she be home soon too?" I asked.

I knew she was in the most serious condition after the accident. Even though she was only burned on twenty percent of her body, she suffered fifth-degree burns from her shoulders up. Her face and head took the brunt of the horrible accident. I heard stories floating around the neighborhood that she woke up from her coma frightened and disoriented, asking for her mother. It tore at my heart.

"Yeah. We all miss her. The whole gang does. We've all missed you guys," Dave said quietly.

"She'll still have months of intensive care in the burn unit. She's not the same anymore...you know that, right?"

David glanced briefly at me then at the ground. "Yeah...I know," he said gravely.

"Davey... She's scared...really scared...she doesn't want anyone to see her. She's worries about what everyone will think. I just want her to be home. I know it will do her good. It will do me good."

I broke the heavy air. "I pray for her every night. I always ask the angels to watch over her," I said with a half-smile.

"She can really use those prayers," Margot said. Her eyes turned glassy as they watered up. Mine did too.

My brother cleared his throat in an attempt to shift the subject. "How did you deal with all that time in the hospital?"

Margot's carefree attitude returned with a chuckle. "I was in a medically induced coma for a couple of weeks. That was the easy part. Boy, was messed I up when they woke me. They must have thought I was crazy, well, crazier than I normally am. They said I kept saying weird stuff."

"Like that crazy lady in the big chair on the Laugh-In show," I said.

"Sorta like that, then I was pretty much bored out of my mind most of the time. I had a lot of time to think, especially about the man who caused the accident."

At the mention of the guy, my brother's gaze narrowed, and he clenched his fists. "Me, too!"

Margot response filled the air with beauty. "Once I came to my senses, I just wanted to give him a hug and forgive him."

My brother was dismayed. "What? Are you kidding me? Forgive that dirtbag? All I've thought about was knocking his head off for you."

Margot placed her hands on David's clenched fists and lowered them. She looked him in the eye with grace and clemency. "I appreciate that, Davey. You've always watched out for me, but I'm at peace with this. *We all* need to be at peace with this."

She pulled us both in for a hug as the tears flowed. "You

know something... I'm just thankful to be alive. God must have some plan for me... I'm just not sure what it is, but I'm gonna spend the rest of my life figuring it out."

Months later, Sarah came home from the intensive care burn unit. My brother and I got word, and we gathered at the end of Blake family's driveway. Margot emerged from her garage and waved to us. The red kite was still hanging in the garage in the same place on the wall behind her. She was wearing a wool knit hat to partially cover her scars. Long dark hair flowed out from under the hat that wraps her face. She ran over to us and hopped in front of my brother.

She ran her fingers through her new hair and flung it in jest like a glamorous movie star. "So, what do you think? It's almost as long as Sarah's used to be. We both got our wigs today, thanks to your mom. She's been such an angel for us. There's a special place in heaven reserved for that woman."

David smirked. "Long hair definitely suits you. I'm likin' it."

Margot peered back toward her house. "Sarah went with a short wig, even shorter than my hair used to be, if you can believe it."

"What? Why?"

"She doesn't want to scare anyone who approaches her from behind if they haven't seen her face. With the short wig, people will at least see the burns on her neck first, before they see...you know..."

"Oh, my God. I'm so sorry. I just thought..."

"It's okay. I'm just so grateful she's finally home."

I was excited Sarah was home. I just wanted to see her. "Me, too!"

"How is she healing up?" my brother asked. He knew just as I did, it was going to be a long road ahead for her and the whole neighborhood. Healing on all levels just takes time, and it was all we had to hold onto now.

"Physically? She's doing much better...but she's still really scared to see everyone. She definitely misses all you guys...I know that for sure."

"Yeah, I figured as much. My mom told me," he replied.

I still had my eyes locked on her house. "Do you think she'll come out today? I really miss her."

"I'm not sure. She wants to see you, but...she thinks she'll scare you. Her face is...uh...not the same. You won't recognize her anymore."

"I don't care what she looks like! She's my friend!"

She leaned into me. "I know. It's just not been easy for her. Since she got home from the hospital the other day, she just spends most of her time in her room. I've barely seen her myself."

My brother eyed the kite in the garage and pointed to it. "She might come out if we can get Dustin to fly that kite. The wind is perfect today."

I screamed in excitement. "Yeah! Can we?" I wanted to see that kite high in the sky, just as much as I wanted to see Sarah.

Margot was reserved. "I don't know...maybe... she's always wanted to see that thing in the air."

David grabbed my shoulder. "You go get the rest of the gang in the neighborhood and meet us in a half-hour. We're gonna need all hands on deck for this one." By the sound of his voice, I knew he'd get that kite in the air no matter what.

I ran off with my brother's mission plans. I felt so important when he trusted me with this task. I wasn't going to fail him either.

David put his arm around Margot and walked her toward her house. "Let's go get Dustin. We're doin' this!"

I rounded up every kid in our neighborhood who had a pulse.

We assembled a decent group of neighborhood kids to prep the kite for a flight. We were all on a mission. On the driveway, there was a box containing many spools of string and a homemade wooden winch.

Some of the kids carefully fed the spools of string onto the winch while I slowly turned the winch handle to wind it on. A couple of the older kids were tying the spools of kite string together to make one massively long string. The girls in the group made ribbons for the tail of the kite. Sarah and Margot's brother, Dustin emerged from the garage carrying a box with more spools of string. He was a tall, lanky guy with short clean-cut dark hair.

"I found some more string in the basement. This should get us near the clouds now." Dustin proudly announced.

"No way! We've got miles of string now," one of the boys yelled.

The girls held up their ribbon creations. "What do you think of the bows? I picked out some ribbon in Sarah's favorite color."

Dustin approved. "Everything is perfect. Just make sure you guys are using the knot I showed you to connect those."

My brother was like a foreman at a construction site. "I've double-checked 'em. They should hold."

I wanted to be recognized for my part too. "I'm winding it on nice and even, jus' like you showed me, too."

Dustin sported a smile for the first time in a long while. "Nice. Keep it steady, guys."

Margot was thrilled too. "You guys are amazing...simply amazing."

It was almost as if our old neighborhood was back to the way used to be. The sun was finally shining us again.

Dustin pointed to the clouds. "We're gonna get this up there today for sure. We have to. We jus' have to."

As the words left his lips, I glanced up at the Blake house and noticed Sarah's slender figure in the main window watching our group. The shadows within the house obscured her so all I could see was her outline. I smiled and shared a small wave with her. She returned a brief wave and then slinked back into the darkness as the curtain fluttered onto the window.

A short time later, David and Margot were at the far end of the street. The kite was ready for its heavenly ascent. There were kids stationed along the string lying on the street. Some of the neighbors, along the route, stepped out onto their front lawns to watch the spectacle unfold. I was proudly operating the winch, awaiting my commands. I held a steady eye on Dustin, who was several feet in front of my rig. He was wearing gloves to protect his hands from the string. My heart was singing with anticipation.

Dustin's voice pierced the air. "Okay, guys! This is how it's gonna work. When I say go, those of you closest to the kite will need to grab the string and start running toward me. Everyone else just keep feedin' them the string until it gets to me. Then I'll take control of it."

We all made a couple of attempts before the kite caught a good breeze and took off. When it did, Dustin yelled out to everyone. "That's it!"

We all cheered. I kept a steady turn on the winch crank feeding string to Dustin. I'd occasionally glance back at the Blake house to see if Sarah would appear, but the yard remained empty of life.

As the kite sailed higher, Dustin had a harder time controlling it, but he was still able to keep it manageable.

Once the kite reached the higher winds, Dustin got concerned. "Davey! Gimme a hand."

I held my thumb up and squinted my eye, covering the kite with the outstretched thumb. It was only a red dot in the sky. Suddenly the string snapped. The kite took off, falling into a wooded area at the top of our street as the remaining string descended from the sky like a drifting spider web.

"Nooooo!!!!!!!" I yelled.

My brother quickly rallied everyone. "Come on guys! Let's go! It's in one of the trees behind old man Smith's house."

I was getting ready to join the group, but Dustin assigned me an important task. "Can you start winding the string back onto the winch? Same as you did earlier today. Just keep it as neat as you can...okay?"

As the group took off running, I yelled out to them. "Do you guys think you can get the kite back?"

My brother turned and mimicked a monkey. "When am I not up for climbing trees?"

I waved him off. "You're such a doofus."

The chatter of the group trailed off, and the neighborhood fell silent again. I started the long, arduous process of winding the string onto the winch.

As I paused to wipe my brow, I noticed Sarah standing in the driveway. Her thin form started to walk toward me slowly. I averted my eyes to the ground and focused intently on winding the string as if not to notice her.

Two thin legs and white sneakers appeared next to me. She had lost weight from her months of intensive care. I stopped winding the string, glanced at the legs, and kept my gaze firmly locked at the ground.

A frail voice broke the air. "I think I can help you with that." It was a voice our neighborhood hadn't heard in many months.

She sounded the same, but the neighborhood had somehow changed. Our street had grown up faster than anyone wanted it to.

"I really missed you."

Sarah knelt down next to me. I kept my gaze locked on the ground, but caught a glimpse of the burn scars on the back of one of her hands when she reached for the string.

Her voice was soothing. "I missed you too. Your mom told me how much you prayed for me. You have no idea how much that means to me."

"I prayed every night for you. I wish your mom was still here."

"I think she's with us all the time now. She taught me faith in God above all else...and I take great comfort in that. That's the gift she gave me. I realize that now more than ever." Her hand gently rested on my back. "I want you to know it doesn't hurt anymore, and at least my temporary nose doesn't fall off now."

"What do you do when you sneeze?"

She poked me. "Well, it's not easy, Mister. I could lose my nose, and who wants to put a nose on that's been in the dirt?"

"Same ol' Sarah," I joked.

She leaned into me and softly said, "I'm still me in here. It's okay to look at me."

I slowly brought my gaze to her eyes. Instead of seeing her disfigurement, I only saw the beauty of her soul. A true appreciation of inner beauty is the gift Sarah gave me that day.

In the precious moment, I learned beauty is not skin deep, it's the deepest part of everything you are—a beautiful divine soul.

An angel holds each of your tears when you're in pain. An angel knows only love and no hate, so don't cry in vain. An angel sees every part of your soul's true inner beauty, so don't ever change who you are. Your most magnificent beauty lies within you.

There is virtually no difference between you and an angel when you love with every essence of your being. Think about it; your soul is pure heavenly love. Every time you share your inner beauty, the very nature of your precious heart, you create a little bit of heaven on earth.

Eleven
FIRST LOVE

"God gives you all the second chances and as much hope as you'll ever need to find what true love is. All you need to do is hold just a little faith."

— Robert Clancy

Is there anything more beautiful in this world than when two hearts come together to become a greater one? The first time I experienced a loving attraction to someone, my soul seemed electrified. My heart was filled with the innate knowledge that love is more than any single heart can ever hold, that's why it's meant to be shared—and I did.

In the fall of 1982, I was a skinny high school Senior who had just risen a bit in popularity. There were four decent rock bands at the high school, and I managed to learn my way around the fretboard to become the lead guitarist of one of them. I was feeling good about my music but struggled with my body image. I had a love-hate relationship with performing in front of others. Although I felt empowered being on-stage, having everyone's eyes on me made me very self-conscious. During that period, you'd almost always find me wearing a

131

black padded Member's Only jacket that hid my thin arms quite well. It was my safety net. Even if it was sweltering, you'd be hard-pressed to find me not wearing that jacket.

In my typical end-of-school routine, I slumped into my regular seat on the school bus, clicked the play button on my Sony Walkman, and slipped on my headphones. I'd spend hours training my ears on the latest guitar solos from the rock gods of the day. I'd hang on every note imagining where it was on the fretboard. I was so lost in my music that I hadn't noticed I'd caught the eye of a slender, athletic blond girl who sat a few seats back from me.

As she exited the bus, her friend handed me a note and pointed to her through the window. As I glanced at her, she blew me a kiss when our eyes met. I quickly turned away in embarrassment. I opened the note. *"I want to get to know you better. Meet me tonight. 8 pm at 1 Compass Court. Love Jay."*

I scanned the crowd of kids for her as the bus engine fired up. She was looking at me straight in the eyes and shot me a flirty smile. Just as fast as she shared a smile, she turned and ran to catch up with her friends. Unfortunately, I wasn't the only one to notice her interest in me.

"Ooh...looks like you got somebody's attention," Dylan blurted out.

I was now beet red in embarrassment, "What?"

"Come on. I totally saw that."

Trying to silence the spectacle, I yelled over to Nate, sitting across from me. "I swear Dylan's got eyes in the back of his head."

Nate was no help, "She's totally into you, dude. A blind man can see that."

"Oh...so that's how it's gonna be...huh, Nate? Thanks for having my back on this one," my voice shuddered in sarcasm.

"Hey...I call 'em like I see 'em. You workin' any nights this week?"

"Yeah, I'll be there Friday night."

Nate and I worked at the same restaurant. I was cleaning tables in the front of the house, and Nate worked in the kitchen. It was my first decent paying job.

"Cool! I'll be there, too. Can you bring a mixtape from your last practice? We recorded most of our jam from last weekend. I can dupe that one for you." I was excited to share recordings of our practice sessions. Nate loved to get the tapes and band updates from me. He always had this genuine enthusiasm for my music.

"Dude, you're like a rock god, and now you got groupies too. I seriously missed the line where they were handing out talent."

Dylan continued to stir the pot, "Apparently that's also the line where they're handing out chicks to rock stars...right Bobbo?"

I folded my arms in disapproval and slumped back into my seat. "You can stop anytime you want."

That night I rode my bike over to Jaydene's house. I was beaming with anticipation. She was sitting on her front steps and strutted over to me before I reached her driveway.

"I wasn't sure if you'd show."

I played coy and let the dance begin, "Let's just say you got my attention."

She was a bit of a spitfire and very forward. Her confidence only threw me further off my game. "Hmmm...looks like this is gonna get interesting. I'm Jay, well, it's actually *Jaydene*, but everyone just calls me Jay."

I was feeling so awkward inside, but my exterior only displayed cool confidence. "I'm Robert, but everyone calls me Bob. Just don't call me Bobby, only my mom does that now."

"Okay, *Mr. Bobby*. Just kidding. I'll call you Bob, I promise. I like that one best," she snickered.

"You better."

"We'll see," she smirked.

"I think you're the first person I ever met named *Jaydene*."

"My mom named me. I always thought it was sorta a combination of mom and dad's names...James and Adrienne, but my dad told me she loved James Dean and named me after him. She also loved Elvis, so I guess I'm lucky I wasn't named *Elvira* or something...and..." Her voice sank a bit. "She died when I was very young. I really only have a few memories of her."

I didn't know what to say. The lexicon of appropriate caring words had evaporated from my mind. "That sucks."

"Yeah, I know. My dad and nan raised me. My nan and I live on this side of the house and my dad lives on the other. So it's mostly jus' me and my nan. My nan keeps him in check...at least she tries to...he's kinda like an older delinquent brother to me."

"Sounds oddly complicated."

"It works for me... and oh, boy, is my nan old-school. I can't tell you how many times she tells me about the perils of those bad boys out there. You're one of them, *right*?"

I sported my most devilish smirk. "Oh, come on. Do I look like a bad boy?"

"Yep, you're just what she warned me about."

"You'll find out soon enough!"

"We'll see," she jabbed. "Other than those nasty boys out there, she pretty much leaves me to my own devices now. I kinda like the independence, if you know what I mean."

"Oh, so you're an *independent girl?*"

She strutted a bit closer to me and patted my chest. "You better believe it. I also do my homework, and let's just say I did my homework on you, too."

"Really? So what's the word on the street about me?"

"I heard you were in that band with Tony and Joe Pallone. My friend, Jackie, told me you guys are pretty good, too."

I had to test our music compatibility meter. "Yeah, I know my way around the fretboard. So what bands are you into?"

"I'm a bit old school. My faves are Led Zeppelin. *I love Robert Plant*, he's my honey. I also have a few albums from The Doors, Janice Joplin and the Stones. Janice reminds me of my mom... especially when I play her song, 'Summertime.' My mom used to sing that to me at my bedtime."

"We're workin' on a couple of Zep songs. You'll have to come to one of our jams."

She pushed me back. "So, you're gonna make me a groupie already?"

We were in a sparring match, and I was outranked. I tried feebly to match her spunk. "If you play your cards right, we might let you hang out."

She was unenthusiastic, "Mm hmm."

I tried to recover, but I was unarmed. "Ummm...Jus' kidding. It'd be cool to have you there." I tried to divert the subject. "Hey, is it alright if I put my bike up by your garage? I'm getting' tired of holdin' this dang thing."

"You might wanna ditch it over by our bushes. Even though my dad says he doesn't care, I know he likes to drive me nuts about his side of the house, and that garage is all his. It's where he used to work on his race car."

"Well, I sure as hell don't wanna get him riled up...and race car?"

I was intrigued by her father. My brother restored a 1967 Convertible Camero. I loved the look of that car, and I hoped to own it one day.

She was matter-of-fact about her father. "Yep, he's a famous race car driver too, well, in his mind he is, and he was, until he had a bad accident. Don't worry, his bark is definitely worse than his bite."

"That's so cool. I bet he's got some stories. I got my eye on my brother's '67 Rally Sport Camero he restored. He'll eventually get bored of it, and it will be all mine one day. I totally can't wait to get my license."

She rolled her eyes. "Don't get him started. He loves to talk about the good ol' days...just about as much as he loves intimidating my boyfriend. So annoying."

At the sound of the word 'b-word,' my love train came to a screeching halt. "I...uh...didn't know you were going out with someone. Maybe I better get goin'."

She burst out laughing. "No, no, no, no! I meant to say, my ex-boyfriend. We broke up a while ago. You're gonna stay right here, at least for a few more minutes." She leaned forward, put her arms around my neck, and gave me a kiss. My face again turned as red a stop sign, but my heart was saying, "Go!"

"Well, okay, then," I announced.

She pressed her forehead on mine and looked lovingly into my eyes. "Now that should put to rest any rumors about me currently havin' a boyfriend, but I think that spot is about to be filled."

Suddenly, the garage door of her house opened. A stocky blond-haired man emerged from the garage holding a large bag. He was unaware of us as he headed to the garbage can on the side of the house to toss the bag.

Jaydene looked over her shoulder at her father with a slight bit of worry written on her face. "You better get goin'. Meet me here Friday night...same time. Here's my number."

As she slipped the note into my jacket pocket, she gave me a quick peck on my cheek. My heart was singing. "I have to work Friday afternoon, but I should be out in time to get over here by then. You can count on it."

"A workin' man, too, huh? I like that. By the way...if my dad likes you, he'll give you an autographed picture of his race car, *The Trip*. That's how you'll know."

I was smiling ear to ear while I began to pedal away. "What's not to like about me?" I announced.

I'd kissed and held hands with a few girls, but this was different. I was in uncharted territory, and my heart was far from the comforts of the shoreline I'd always known. I was wading into the ocean of love.

I couldn't wait until Friday. That whole week I was walking on air. I loved the feeling of someone being interested in me. I had a newly-found confidence I'd never felt before. I was worth something.

That Friday, I rolled up to work on my bike. Nate was hanging with a couple of the older guys. They were taking a smoking break in back of the building. All of them were wearing stained white aprons, ripped jeans, and work boots. I was a front-house staffer, so in contrast, I was wearing a white dress shirt, a thin black tie, khaki pants, and dress shoes. Our two groups didn't often mix unless it was for nefarious reasons. I steered clear and waved Nate over to me.

"Yo, Nate! I got it dude!" I proudly held up a cassette tape.

"Cool! Is that from your last practice?"

"Yeah. It's got a couple of Zeppelin songs were workin' on, 'Iron Man' and a Def Leppard tune off their High 'n' Dry album."

"Cool! You playin' lead on any of these?"

I always drank in Nate's enthusiasm for my guitar skills. "Oh yeah! I just about learned the entire solo for 'Heartbreaker' too."

He snatched the tape from my hand. "No way! That totally smokes!"

"Dude... I've been practicing...a lot...'till my fingers are practically bleeding. Catch this...I almost saved up enough cash to get a Marshall hundred-watt head too!"

"Sweet! You're definitely gonna kick some ass at the Battle of the Bands this year."

I pumped my fist in agreement. "No doubt!"

"I wish I had your talent, man. But alas...I will only be a purveyor of the rock gods," he graciously relented.

As I poked Nate, one of the kitchen guys flicking a cigarette butt at the dumpster caught my eye. I observed him taking a small plastic bag out of his pocket and stealthily slipping it into the waiting hand of the other guy. Money was exchanged on the sly with a handshake before they headed back into the kitchen.

I folded my arms in discernment. "Do I have to keep my eye on you? Some of those dudes you're hangin' with look a bit shady."

"What, you front-house staffers think you're too good for us kitchen dregs?" Nate scoffed.

"You know what I mean. I know what goes on back here. You're a bit smarter than being a kitchen lifer. Just stay away from the drugs, dude."

"I'm cool. No worries. We're mostly just talkin' bands, crazy parties, chicks, and stuff."

Suddenly, I realized I was running late for work. "Oh crap, I got go clock in or Mr. Maiden will be ridin' my ass tonight. They don't call him *Iron Maiden* for nothin', ya know!"

Nate gave me a knuckle bump. "Catch ya later, dude...and thanks for the tape. I'm workin' the fryer tonight. I'll leave you some fries on the break room shelf for you at seven-thirty. You know I take care of my peeps."

"Thanks. dude!"

"Hey...I almost forgot...did you hook up with that chick from the bus or what?"

"Let's just say it's gettin' interesting."

He waved his finger at me. "I knew she had the hots for you. So, you goin' for those younger girls now? She's a sophomore, right?"

"Yep," I smirked.

"You cradle robber," he taunted.

"Whatever, dude."

He just shook his head. "I don't know if I can keep up with you, man. Rock god, groupies—where does it end?"

"Let's hope it doesn't. I think I could get quite used to this."

"Like I said, you're a rock star."

I sprang into the restaurant lobby smiling ear to ear. A waitress, Josie, and the cashier, Beatrice, were at the cash stand. They both looked up as I bounced in. Josie had a very earthy air about her. Her long, straight brown hair was always pulled back into a ponytail, accentuating her demure kindness.

Beatrice immediately jammed her thumb at me. "Get a load of this one...looks he's got some extra pep in his step tonight, huh? I'd say someone is in love."

"Yep, definitely love," Josie sighed.

"So, do tell," Beatrice prodded.

I tried to sidestep her. "What?"

"I've been around the block long enough to know. So, what's her name?"

"Come on! Give it up," Josie jabbed.

I caved to their inquisition. "Okay, okay! *It's Jaydene.* I barely know her. We just met."

"Looks like you got to know her well enough."

Beatrice sighed and settled into the cash stand counter. "I bet he kissed her."

My face began to burn with a crimson tide of embarrassment. "God...I can't get away with anything in here with you two on the case."

Beatrice's laugh rang across the lobby. "I knew it! He's smitten."

"Ahhh, love in the air," Josie jested.

I pursed my lips, and sighed.

"You guys are worse than my sister. I gotta clock in."

My shift finally ended, and my heart was pumping with anticipation. I couldn't get on my bike fast enough to get to Jaydene's house. As I pulled into her driveway, she was again waiting for me.

"Hmmm...I wasn't sure if you'd show," she joked.

"Who, me? Well, I didn't have anything else goin' on tonight, so I thought I'd ride around your neighborhood...and...well... here I am."

"Well then...It looks like you found somethin' goin' on."

"Maybe."

As I started toward the bushes to stow my bike, she surprised me when she said, "You can put that up by the garage."

"Are you sure? What about your dad?"

"He wants to meet you."

My heart skipped a beat. "Tonight?"

"Yep! He loves fast cars, the Yankees, and of course me. If you talk about only lovin' the first two things, you'll be just fine."

My thoughts dropped like a deck of cards. I struggled to pick them up.

"That could be a challenge since I kinda love all three. And uh, you're a Yankees fan too? That's so cool. My favorite team since like second grade."

"Well, I was born a Yankees fan. Sounds like you got a late start."

"Maybe. But I catch up quick," I said, smirking.

"I think he wanted a son, so he taught me how to play baseball. I ain't no ordinary girl, you know."

"Then, I better make a good impression. So let me get this straight—you like cool cars, the Yankees, awesome bands, *and you play baseball*? You're like the perfect girlfriend. Are you sure you're for real?"

She rolled her eyes. "Come on." She grabbed my hand and pulled me into her house.

The walls of her room were covered with posters of Led Zeppelin, Janice Jopin, The Rolling Stones, The Doors, and Bucky Dent. Bucky was the New York Yankees hero who hit the fabled home run in the 1978 AL East tiebreaker against the Red Sox at Fenway Park. As she passed his poster, she kissed her hand and tapped his lips with it.

"I jus' love this guy."

On her dresser stood a small picture of her mother holding her in her arms. She looked to be about two or three years old in the photo. A couple of promo photos of her father's race car were taped to her closet door. A small love seat was next to her bed with a television across from it. Various rock music albums were stacked next to a stereo record player. Her dog, Sandy, a tan Shepard and Beagle mix, was lying on the edge of the bed.

I was slightly uncomfortable being in a girl's bedroom, but her décor put me at ease.

"So this is your pad, huh? You're a bit cooler than you let on. I like it," I said. My head swiveled around to take in the entire surroundings.

"I've got everything a girl needs in here...my own phone, cable TV, music...and you."

I blushed a bit and tried to cover my reddened face by petting her dog.

"And who's this old guy?"

"That's Sandy. He's getting a bit green in the gills these days. He's, like, older than dirt, but I love him."

"You're not exactly like the other girls I know."

"I'm the only girl you need to know."

"I like a girl who knows what she wants."

I tried my best to be coy, but for this dance of the hearts, I didn't know any good steps.

"You have a seat right there. I've got some popcorn in the works, and a scary movie on HBO lined up for us."

Before dropping into the couch, I grabbed the picture of her and her mother. "Is this your mom?"

"That's my favorite picture in the world," she replied, her voice softening. "It's one of the last pics of me and her together."

I looked intently at the photo. "She's so beautiful. She looks a lot like you. What happened? Was she sick?" Before I could retract my question, I saw the answer written on her face.

"I really don't like to talk about it. I don't remember much because I was so young," she slowly answered, her voice was shaking.

I set the picture down, stood up, and took her hands into mine. "It's okay. I'm here for you."

"I really don't ever talk about this. I don't even know why I'm telling you this. I trust you I guess...she um...took her life... over there on the other side of the house. I guess that's why he likes me to stay on this side."

I pulled her in for a hug. "Oh, my God. I'm so sorry. That's horrible."

"She was sick. I don't know the whole story. I used to blame myself."

"It's not your fault. I hope you know that."

"Yeah, I know." She sank deeper into the comfort of my arms. "You're amazing."

I didn't have a framework for how to handle the emotions of this moment. I only knew of one other person who took his life, but I was shielded from the raw emotions of the terrible incident. I just did my best to change the subject. "I think we need to get the movie on...we need to get our minds in another place."

She looked into my eyes for a moment and shared a small

smile with me. "Yeah...and our hearts."

There was tenderness in her voice that made my heart swell.

"Oh, I think they're heading right where they need to be goin'. You know I'm not that cool or popular, right? So why do I deserve someone as amazing as you?"

Her head rested on my heart. "I'm not sure if I deserve you."

A short time later, we were sitting close together on her couch eating popcorn. We were totally engrossed in the horror film. Only the light of the television illuminated our faces. I'd managed to work my arm around her shoulder. We were unaware of the stocky figure standing in her doorway.

"Herrrhem!"

I nearly jumped out of my skin. Popcorn flew everywhere. "Oh...um...hey sir. Nice to meet you. You, like, totally scared me." I quickly flicked the bedroom lights on and extended my hand for a handshake.

"Looks like you were doing just fine there," said Jay.

He smirked at Jaydene. She showed her displeasure.

'Now I know where she gets it from,' I thought. 'Yep, she's a pistol, alright.'

"Really dad?"

As much as Jaydene dished it, she didn't seem to like the same sense of humor being served to her.

As Jay shook my hand, he said, "Are you sure you're ready for this one? She's got one hell of a fast engine and no brakes."

146

I grinned.

His comment only served to make her more perturbed. "Dad! Stop!"

"Just kidding. I love to get a good rise outta her when I can. I'll leave you guys to your movie. She just wanted me to meet you...that's all."

I struggled to regain my composure and pointed to his race car pic. "I love your ride. Drag racing, right?"

"Yep, and that's the only kind of racing there is. So Jay said you're looking at a Camaro. What year?"

My shoulders relaxed a bit. "It's a '67 with a 357 and four on the floor. It needs a little engine work, but the body is in decent shape. My brother restored it."

"Sounds nice...bring it by when you get it, and I'll help you tune it up. I got a whole mechanics area built into this ol' house."

"Really? That's awesome!" I was excited.

Jaydene was less enthused. "Thanks, Daddy! You can go home now."

"Nightie, night, Sweetie," he said in the most sarcastic tone he could muster. Then he turned to me. "Nice meeting you... you're a good kid."

"He can be so annoying sometimes," Jaydene said under her breath.

"Well, I thought he was pretty cool."

A couple of minutes later, Jay came back to her room.

He was holding an autographed picture of his race car and handed it to me. "I thought you might like this."

"Wow! Thanks!"

He flicked off the bedroom lights and headed back down the hallway. "Enjoy the movie you two. I'm goin' to bed."

"I think he likes you," she said softly. Her arms wrapped around my neck. "Now, where were we?"

We fell back onto her couch passionately kissing each other. Yes. Beatrice was right. I was smitten.

Wandering in the wonderment of love doesn't mean you're lost; it means you've found a beautiful place to get lost within. Love is the precious garden of your life. It's the place where your soul grows with every waking moment. Just like any garden, love needs to be tended to. What's growing in your heart today?

No one will ever know who you truly are until you raise the curtains of your heart while you sing and dance to the sweet melodies of love on the stage of life. Living in full expression of who you are, and who you are meant to be takes courage, but it also takes acceptance of your true self. How can you expect others to love you when you haven't shown them who to love? Accept yourself, and others will accept the *true you*.

TWELVE
THREE WORDS

"God gives you all the second chances and as much
hope as you'll ever need to find what true love is.
All you need to do is hold just a little faith."

— *Robert Clancy*

All journeys of the heart contain valleys of despair and mountains of hope. To survive the trip, you need to realize that the heavens are always above those valleys, and the mountaintops touch them. To reach the summit, you have to take one hope-filled step past all of your fears, doubts, and worries. I found that all of the trials and tribulations you endure are meant to show you just how resilient your precious soul is.

Jaydene and I quickly became a noted couple in high school. Other than when I was practicing with my band, I spent every waking minute with her. She was my best friend. Our relationship consumed my world.

It was a typical day at school, and I was heading to class flanked by Nate and Dylan. Suddenly, two boys from the sophomore class came up from behind and shoulder bump me as they passed. Pat was the larger of the two. Danny seemed shy and looked somewhat like me, just a bit shorter.

Nate immediately responded to the duo. "Yo, Danny, why don't you and your sasquatch watch where you're going?"

"Whatever, dude," Pat said, spewing attitude. Then he pointed directly at me "Maybe he should watch where he's going or maybe I'll do a little remodeling on his face. You think you're cool or something with that guitar?"

Danny pushed Pat away from our group. "Come on, Pat. He's not worth it."

"Damn sophomores! They think they're running the school already," Dylan exclaimed, then he turned his attention to Pat and Danny and fired off a parting shot at them. "Run along, children. You'll inherit this dump next year while I'm out running the world."

Pat and Danny walked backward for a short stint. Pat gave me a menacing glare before he finally turned around.

I threw my arms up in the air. "You know those two doofs? What the hell did I do to them?"

"Yeah, I've seen them around. I think that dude, Danny, got an electric guitar...probably not as cool as yours, though. Maybe they're jealous, or I guess you're just popular, Mr. Rock Star," Nate said. He attempted to charlie horse my arm to emphasize his point.

"Yeah, but I didn't paint a target on my back!?
What the hell!"

I was angry, but I was also confused. For the most part, I got along with everyone at the school. I didn't understand why I was targeted. I brushed off the incident.

"Nate's right. It's plain and simple jealousy."

I regained my composure and headed for my physics class. Like clockwork, Jaydene sneaked up on me from behind and grabbed my arm. Our class schedules often put us at opposing sides of the school. This was one of the few times I could see her in the hallway.

She pulled me close and whispered in my ear. "I wrote you a *special note.*" She gave me a seductive wink and slipped the note into my hand.

Just as I began to share my smile with her, Dylan suddenly poked his head in between our heads while he wrapped his arms around us. "Ooh...love notes. Is it a marriage proposal?"

"You're such a jackass, Dylan," Jaydene quickly countered.

Dylan straightened himself up, and his eyes blazed a bit. "What? I already know I'm marrying Crystal."

Whenever Dylan was serious about something, his eyes would give his heart away. I was just worried about passing the SATs, and Dylan was planning his entire life.

"Dude! Shouldn't you graduate first?"

"I'm gonna get hitched after graduation, numb nuts," Dylan said in his effervescent smart-ass tone. He turned to Jaydene to prove his case. "You know when it's meant. Crystal and me... yeah, we're for life."

At the top of the list of couples voted most likely to fail were Dylan and Crystal's names. They would argue with each other over nonsense things in the morning, break up by noon and then be back together again before the day was out.

Suddenly, the school bell rang out. Dylan grabbed our shoulders and pushed us together. "I'll leave you two love birds to your wedding bells."

"Not today! Mr. Wright is gonna kill me. This is gonna be my third late to his class," Jaydene exclaimed as she sprinted down the hallway.

I was the last student to grab my desk, and this was not the class to be late for. Mr. Warner, one of the strictest teachers in the school, expected everyone to be ready to go at the sound of the bell.

My brother, David, was in his class a few years back, and he plowed a beautiful wide path of infamy for me to follow. On my first day of class, Mr. Warner's paused when he called out my last name during attendance.

"Clancy," he growled. "Where's Clancy?"

I slowly raised my hand.

"I've got my eye on you, Mister," he said firmly. "You're the brother of that David Clancy, aren't you? I know all about you."

I tried to quell his inquisition. "I'm not like him. I study and stuff."

The torment my brother put him through was too much to overcome his preconditioned foul opinion of me.

My brother once wore an off-color t-shirt to his class. Mr. Warner asked him to turn it inside out. When my brother refused, Mr. Warner threatened him.

"Suppose I call your mother and tell her about that nasty shirt you're wearing."

Sarcasm bled from his lips.

"Go ahead. My mother bought it for me."

Mr. Warner steamed.

I tried to fly under the radar in that class, but he always had his eyes firmly fixed on me.

"Well, everyone. It looks like we can get started with today's lesson. *Mr. Clancy* has finally graced us with his presence."

Slowly, I took out my book while Mr. Warner began the lesson. I fell quickly into a bit of a daydream while I gazed down at the note in my hand. It said, "For your eyes only (Heart) Jay." When I tried to hide it under my book, Mr. Warner snatched it out of my hands.

"So, what do we have here? Shall I share this with the entire class Mr. Clancy?"

My heart was in my throat. "No. God, no."

Mr. Warner carefully unfurrowed the note, put on his reading glasses, and proceeded to read it to himself. He muttered the words under his breath, and his expression appeared quite amused at some of the note's highlights.

"Well, class...it appears that Mr. Clancy is a wonderful baseball player who might attempt to round third base this weekend with a young lady friend. It also appears that he's quite proficient in French...ummm...kissing that is."

The entire class giggled.

"Shall I share this wonderful prose with the entire class, Mr. Clancy," he taunted.

I turned cherry red. "Please, Mr. Warner. No. Please, don't read it out loud."

He handed the note back to me. My sigh of relief could be heard in the next county.

"Maybe if you were a little more focused on *physics* rather than getting, shall we say, *physical*, your grade might improve a bit."

I quickly stowed the note in my backpack and went limp as the class erupted in laughter.

The day Jaydene earned her driver's permit, she also got her first set of wheels. I pulled into her driveway to find her father proudly standing next to a 1969 maroon Chevy Chevelle. She was in the driver's seat.

I jumped out of my car in excitement and ran over to her. "You passed the permit test?"

"Yep, I got a perfect score, and this little baby is my new ride," she said, as she hopped out and patted the hood of the muscle car.

"That totally smokes," I exclaimed.

She was smiling ear to ear.

"I can practice for my driver's test when I take Nan to the grocery store."

Her father coughed in jest. "To be quite honest, I'm not sure how you're gonna pass your road test with that lead foot of yours. The apple never falls far from the tree, I guess."

"I learned it all by watching you," she retorted.

"You're just lucky Nan can't see that well, or you'd put her in an early grave," he countered immediately.

Jaydene rolled her eyes.

Jay ignored her and patted the hood of the car.

"Let's get her tuned up and see what's goin' on in there. It sounds like she's got a slight timing issue."

"And my girl needs some fresh oil," Jaydene added.

As fast as the words left her lips, she jumped into the driver's seat and blazed the Chevelle over the garage pit area. The wheels graced the edges of the pit, which made her father cringe.

His arms flailed in disapproval.

"Easy there, lead foot!"

"Seriously? I know what I'm doing," she whipped back.

"And that's the part that keeps me up at night and drinking the Wild Turkey."

She rolled her eyes again as he returned his attention to the idling car.

"Do you hear that tick...that's the timing belt...probably

because of the low oil pressure, but it's not too bad. First, we need to change out these spark plugs, then deal with the oil."

He pulled the oil dipstick, wiped it down with a rag, and rechecked it.

"Yep, she's low and definitely needs an oil change. We'll get her purring in no time."

I was drinking in all the tips on car engines he doled out. I loved every minute of it. When he finished the tune-up, he wiped his hands with a rag and tossed it onto one of the large red tool chests.

"That about does it. You just need to put in a new oil filter and refill the oil. Five quarts should do it."

"I just gotta say thanks for all this. I learned a lot."

"I should be thanking you. I love working on these old muscle cars." He tossed the old oil filter to Jaydene and motioned for her to go to the basement storage area. "Can you show him where I keep the oil and the spare filters in the basement. I'm sure I got one down there that fits this. Just match the number on this one."

"Sure." She grabbed my hand and pulled me toward the basement. "Come on. You're gonna love this."

The walls of the basement were lined with shelves packed with various automotive parts. I was in awe of how many car parts were down there.

"Whoa! This place is like an automotive parts store."

"Not sure why he's still hanging on to all this stuff. I think he still dreams of racing again, and that ain't gonna happen."

"Well, I'm glad he's kept this stuff. This place is a goldmine!"

"Yeah...if you think so. I think it's a bunch of crap."

"Are you kidding? He's got just about everything we'd ever need for our cars down here."

"At least something good will come outta here." She guided me to the far side of the basement. "This type of oil filter should be...hmmm...over there somewhere."

I scoured the shelf intently for the filter. The boxes were covered in a thin layer of dust. I had to wipe them with my hand to see the part numbers on them.

"I don't think anyone has touched these in a few years," I said as I dusted my hands.

"Since my mom died, he doesn't come down here much anymore. She always loved to help him get parts from here."

"Yeah...understandable."

"Wait...I think this is the one."

As I grabbed the box, I accidentally bumped the shelf, and a few boxes fell haphazardly onto the floor.

"Crap! I'm such a klutz."

I scrambled to pick up the filter boxes, not noticing that one of them was filled with 45 caliber bullet rounds. They spilled out onto the floor and began to roll everywhere. At first, I thought they were bolts, but once I figured out what they were, I yelled out in surprise.

"Hey! What the hell are those doing in there?"

As the words left my mouth, I spun around saw a bullet round slowly roll up to Jaydene's feet. She momentarily glanced at the bullet, then into my eyes before collapsing to the ground in a devastating emotional heap.

"It's how she did it... it's how she did it...it's how she did it... it's how she..."

"Jay! Oh my God! I had no idea. I'm so sorry. I'm so sorry. I didn't mean to."

I felt horrible that I opened this awful pain in her heart. I didn't know how to help her. I felt so emotionally lost in that moment. I rushed over to her and wrapped my arms around her. It was in that horrible moment that the three words left my lips.

"I love you."

She sank into my arms. I just held her to my heart on that basement floor until she stopped crying. It's the first time I'd ever spoken those three words to her in the context of being committed to her. My heart was changed. I entered uncharted territory in the sea of love.

***

The deep pain from the loss of someone dear to you causes waves of grief to fall upon your soul like sheets of sorrowful rain. Just know that one day, you'll be able to dance in that rain while you await the sun to dry your tears. There's a break in every storm of the heart. It's not that you get through grief; it's more so that it becomes part of you—it becomes only love within your heart.

You may also rest assured that the sun will always rise over the ashes of every broken life. When you trust in the big picture, the winds of faith will carry those ashes to a place of renewal. When it does, allow hope to be a seed that's planted firmly on this new ground. It will grow when you nourish it with love, for this is how you grow strong again.

Thirteen
REQUIEM

*"Alone in the blackness of a starless night, I
could only call upon grief's dark cloak to cover
my shivering soul. Time's essence passed as an
endless sea of sorrow that washed over me. Every
unbearable wave that broke upon my shore carried
but a few of my tears out to that desolate abyss."*

— Robert Clancy

The deep pain from the loss of someone dear to you causes
waves of grief to fall upon your soul like sheets of sorrowful
rain. Just know that one day, you'll be able to dance in that
rain while you await the sun to dry your tears. There's always a
break in every storm of the heart.

In the spring of 1983, my band was one of the four selected
for the Battle of the Bands. The center of the gym was filled
with more than half the school. Each group set up on makeshift
stages along each side of the gym. I was excited and nervous,
but knew my band had a decent playlist, and a good singer. One
of the downfalls of most bands is they had excellent musicians
but lacked a good front man. Luckily, we had one of the two best

161

front men the school could offer. Jaydene was in the center in the crowd, ready to cheer us on.

At this point in our relationship, unfortunately I'd become very possessive of her. I would get upset when her friends wanted to do something with her. I'd get frustrated when they called her while I was hanging at her house. I tried to force her to quit sports, so she'd have more time for me. I was jealous beyond measure. I wanted to be the center of her attention. This disparity often sparked heated arguments between us.

This unwanted emotional guest moved into my heart—jealousy. I struggled to communicate what was going on inside me, but it was like trying to play music on a broken piano. Half of the keys were missing on my emotional piano, and the love song I was trying to play for Jaydene was way out of tune with her. Our relationship became rocky, and we struggled to hold it together.

My band was mid-set in our playlist when I noticed Danny working his way through the crowd toward Jaydene. When he reached her, he appeared to be upset and attempted to hold her hand a couple of times. She was embarrassed by his advances and pushed him back. The spectacle caused me to mess up my guitar solo. Our bass player was less than amused.

"Come on, man! Get it together!"

I responded with a frustrated look and nodded toward Jaydene. The bass player watched her head out of the crowd with the Danny and his friend Pat in tow. They hung in the corner of the gym, where they appeared to be arguing. Danny and Pat left the gym in a huff when Jaydene headed back into the crowd. The bass player rolled his eyes in disapproval.

"Chicks will always bring you down, dude. You're a marked man now."

I just shook my head. I didn't want to deal with yet another issue, but my stewpot of jealousy was about to boil over. After the concert, Jaydene stood by me while I packed up my gear. I didn't say a word to her. The expression written on my face said it all.

When I reached my car, I flopped my guitar case carelessly into my car trunk, slammed the lid, and hopped into the driver's seat. Jaydene appeared embittered by my jealous antics. My heart was enraged.

"They almost kicked me out of the band tonight. So, can you tell me what the hell is going on?"

"With what?"

"Come on," I yelled. "I saw you with that guy, Danny, and his gorilla, Pat. What the hell is he doing with you?"

"He's my ex...It's complicated."

My heart sank like the Titanic. The car filled with an icy, desolate ocean between our hearts. My brain was no longer connected to my mouth. I struggled to contain my emotions.

"Complicated? It didn't look complicated to me! I don't want you talkin' to him."

"He just wants to be friends, that's all."

Anger welled up in my heart.

"I could give a rat's ass. I don't care! I'm your *friend*!

I'm *your boyfriend*, or did you forget that?"

"You don't control me! No one does," she yelled.

Our emotional walls rose to an all-time new height, and this only served to enrage me more. The mercury of anger blasted through the top of my emotional thermometer. I was no longer in control of myself. I punched the steering wheel.

"Why the hell are you doing this to me?" I screamed.

"It's you! You're pushing me away with your insane jealousy! Don't you see that?" she shouted.

She was right. I just couldn't see through my emotional fog of that moment, and I didn't want to take the blame. I punched the steering wheel again, then abruptly started the car and revved the engine, before angrily throwing it into gear. The tires tore up the gravel and spit it out like my shredded heart. She turned away from me.

I awoke numb the next morning and stayed in bed most of the day. I was scared, frustrated, and above all, upset with myself. I wanted to turn life off and push a do-over button, but life just keeps going. I was forced to get ready for my late afternoon work shift. I didn't want to speak to anyone. When I entered the restaurant's kitchen that day, I tried to shuffle past Nate. He knew immediately something was wrong.

"What's up with you? You look like your cat just died or somethin', dude."

"Rough night," I groveled.

Nate did his best air guitar solo in an attempt to cheer me up.

"You sounded pretty good to me. Second place in the Battle of the Bands isn't the end of the world, you know."

"It's not that, it's Jay. Something's way off." I shook my head. "I don't know, dude."

"Well, I gotta cure for that. Tommy and I are gonna catch that band, Switchblade, at the new place up in Saratoga tomorrow night. Why don't you hang with us?"

I probably would have taken him up on his offer any other night, but this was the worst argument Jaydene and I had ever had. The previous night consumed my soul. I just kept going over everything in my mind, and that only made it worse.

"Nah...I gotta straighten things out with Jay."

I continued past Nate to hang my jacket up. When I got to the end of the kitchen, Nate called me out.

"Your loss, dude. Chicks over music? I'm disappointed in you. Did you at least bring me that mix tape you promised me?

I smirked at him in frustration and sharply flipped him off.

"Exactly my point," he yelled.

The minutes dragged on that night. I must have looked at the clock a thousand times before my seemingly endless shift finally concluded. My mind was racing, and I wanted my heart to get off the rollercoaster. I rushed to Jaydene's house. When I got there, I closed my eyes and waited a minute before ringing her doorbell.

"Please, God. Please make her understand." I prayed.

Slowly, she answered the door. Her face was riddled with

the strife I'd painted upon it. Shame welled up in me for how I treated her. I just wanted it all to go away. I was on a runaway train heading into the abyss. I struggled for the right words when I flopped onto her couch.

"I care Jay, I do."

She crossed her arms.

"You can't tell me who I can be friends with. You got mad that time when I went shopping with Jackie...then you get pissed when any of my friends call me."

"I know...but...I don't trust that guy Danny...and..."

Her eyes narrowed. *"And me?* You don't *trust me?"*

"That's not what I'm saying...you know what I mean," I said in a feeble attempt to defend myself.

"I don't."

The distance between us felt like the Grand Canyon. I was desperately grasping for the edge, but there was nothing there to hold onto. I fell into a huge hole that was widening within my heart.

"I just want things to go back to the way they were. Can't we just make this stop? Please...I'm begging you. I can change."

I attempted to take her hands in mine, but she pushed them away.

"Jay...please! Don't do this."

"I need time. Maybe we need time...apart."

I lowered my head in anguish and walked out of her

room to my car. I desperately wanted her to chase after me. No emotional recuse party was deployed. I was alone in the wilderness, and I drove off.

Hours passed before I parked my car angrily in my driveway. I sat there for a few minutes in my clouded thoughts before walking over to Dylan's house. I needed help. Surely Dylan would have some plan on how to circumnavigate this awful situation. After all, he and Crystal broke up nearly every day.

Dylan always had a quirky sense of humor and a unique perspective on situations. I needed his advice. That night we ended up walking around his neighborhood before ending up in our old elementary schoolyard lying on our backs looking up at the stars.

"Remember when life was so simple here?" Dylan asked. "We had nothin' to worry about in the world."

"Yeah, I do...the worst thing that could happen then was Herman Munster, and even he was cool in the end. Those days are now over. Chicks are just messed up. Everything was so perfect. I don't even know what to do. I screwed up everything with her."

"No doubt! Crystal pulled some crazy crap on me too, and now she needs some time to figure us out again? I can't figure that girl out. She's my whole life. I really love her."

"Dude, I can't handle the 'L' word now. I'm frustrated outta my friggin' mind! Jay is pretty much my whole world, and now it's upside down."

"I'd have Crystal talk to her, but she just hangs up on me. I've been through this before. Just give it time. She'll come around. It's gotta be the hormones or something."

"I don't know. This is different somehow. I messed up bad and said some dumbass things. She's way pissed at me."

"Give it time, dude."

"Time is about all I have right now. Time to think about everything I could've or should've done."

The next day I dragged myself to work at a turtle's pace and was nearly twenty minutes late. I didn't care. I didn't want to be around people. I just wanted to retreat to my ivory tower until the dark clouds lifted off my life. I parked my car haphazardly and was greeted by a kitchen guy on a cigarette break out back.

"You're late, dude! Ol' Man Maiden is lookin' for your ass," he said. "And dude, I thought you should know that, uhhh..."

I brushed him off and kept my snail's pace toward the entrance. Josie and Beatrice were at the cash stand as usual, but their solemn disposition grabbed my eye. I knew I was going to get the hammer for being late. Josie reached out and stopped me when I attempted to pass her.

"Hey! I need to talk to you about something," she said somberly.

"I know...I'm late...and I didn't do a great job on cleaning up the other day. I'm dealing with some stuff. I'll do better tonight. I promise."

"It's not that. It's Nate."

"Come on...I can't be responsible for him too," I pleaded. "He's his own man."

"He's gone," she said.

"What? He quit? Why?" I seethed.

I tried to push past her while my thoughts raced. "This is just what I need. He was one of the few people I look forward to seeing at this dump!"

Josie's voice dropped to a somber pitch. "No...there was a horrible car accident last night. His friend Tommy fell asleep at the wheel...and Nate...he didn't make it. I'm sorry. I'm really sorry."

I cracked a half smile and looked past her. "This isn't funny. Did Mr. Maiden put you up to this? Come on... he's here. I have the mixtape I made for him...he's..."

Josie took my hands into hers as a tear ran down her cheek. "I'm so sorry. I really am. He was a good person."

I felt her sadness course up my arms and over my heart like a dark, cold blanket of grief. I collapsed into one of the lobby chairs.

I was angry at myself. I was angry at life. I was angry at God.

"No, this isn't real," my heart begged. "Why is this happening to me? Why? Why Nate?" I mumbled. The tears dripped from my fingers. Each one seemed like a footnote for my horrible life.

Nate's wake was a few days later. As I entered the funeral home, two girls from my high school passed me. They were both crying uncontrollably. I moved further into the funeral home corridor, and the bass player from my band exited the casket room. He averted his eyes as he passed me. His face was a gravestone of anguish. My heart sank.

The room was filled with the sorrow of a thousand rainy days as I walked up to Nate's lifeless body. His hands were gently folded, clasping a simple set of rosary beads. It was a peaceful slumber from which I wished with all my heart he would awaken. I stood there numb for a minute before my legs buckled and I collapsed kneeling in front of his casket. I closed my eyes as the tears welled up in them. I said the Lord's Prayer quietly to myself then I prayed for Nate's soul.

"Please God, please take Nate into heaven. He's a good person. He was a good friend. Please watch over him and his family."

How often does a distressing event in your life make you say, "God! Why would you do this to me?" The perspective you need to take is not what *God does to you*, but what *God does with you* in divine grace and love that defines what your soul is. Everything that happens in life does have a reason, and the mystery is simple to solve. It's always been about one thing—love.

FOURTEEN
ROCK BOTTOM

"Even when you hit rock bottom, God's loving light still shines down upon you. You just need to lift your weary chin up high enough to see it."

— Robert Clancy

L ove is the thread that holds the very fabric of the universe together...and sometimes it seems to be all that's holding your world together. When you fall out of love, they don't tell you that there's no one there to catch you. Sometimes you have to hit rock bottom to come to the realization that God was holding you the whole time.

Over the coming weeks, several of my work shifts would end with me pleading with Jaydene on the lobby payphone. I felt like the rug holding my life together had been ripped out from under it. She was the only person I could turn to, and I'd destroyed her heart with the one thing I couldn't fix...*me.*

"Jay, I can change... I'll be better... You'll see," I implored.

"You hurt me. Don't you see that?"

"Just let me see you. I need to see you."

171

"When? Tonight? No!"

"Yes. Tonight," I pleaded.

"No. I need space. You need to give me my space."

"Come on, Jay! I don't understand. That doesn't make any sense."

"You've been nothing but out of control with your raging jealousy, and you won't even admit it," she rebuked.

"Alright...I'll admit it then."

"It's too late for that."

"I'll say it then...*I'm jealous.*"

Her wall grew between us. "I don't know. I don't trust you anymore."

"But this is important. I need to..."

"Give me time. Can't you just do that?"

I tried my best to quell the emotional stew, but it had already boiled over.

"I...love you. It's all I can say...It's all I have left. I'll see you, later...okay?"

The phone went icy cold in a deafening silence.

"Jay? Jay? Hello?"

I slammed the phone onto the receiver. As I passed the cash stand, Beatrice pretended to look busy as if she didn't overhear my phone call. I jumped into my car and sped off to Jaydene's house. As my car rounded the corner, I was stunned to find her standing with Danny and Pat in her garage. I pulled into the driveway behind Pat's car and jumped out. Jaydene motioned for Danny and Pat to remain in the garage as she briskly walked toward me. Fittingly for the moment, a light rain began mixing with the tears flowing down my cheeks.

"What the hell is this? What the hell is going on?" I shouted. I was panicked.

"You can't be here," she said. "You need to go."

"No, no, no...this isn't happening."

Pat taunted from the garage. "More like it's already happened, douchebag. You heard her, time for you to leave. My man, Danny, here has her in good hands if you know what I mean."

"Shut it, Pat. Let me handle this," she reprimanded. "It's not like that!"

My emotional rollercoaster jumped the tracks.

"Are you with him now? How long, Jay? How long?"

"It's not like that. You just gotta go, okay. You just can't be here. Please give me space."

"You can't do this! You can't do this to me! Come on, Jay! I need you," I screamed.

Jay emerged from the house and stood between us. He motioned for her to go into the garage.

"You can't do this here. You're a good kid...you are." Momentarily, he glanced back at Jaydene as if to try to make sense of the situation. He could only shake his head. "Things are just different now...she uh...she's with someone else now,

I think. You gotta go. You just gotta go. I can't have this going on in my driveway." His tone lowered to heartfelt drawl. He could see the pain rising from my heart into my eyes. "I wish it was different, kid. I do."

I surrendered to the hopelessness of the moment. I backed away, despondent, dropped into my car, and slowly pulled away. Pat mocked me as I drove off.

The rain flashed into a torrential downpour. It matched the storm of pain raging in my soul. I was broken. It felt like a thousand daggers piercing my crumbling heart all at once. I couldn't function. Every time I tried to move, waves of sorrow coursed through my body. I was crying uncontrollably.

It was hours later when I finally entered my house. I was beyond emotionally drained. I hated the feeling, and I hated myself. The television flicker illuminated the living room as I slipped passed my father, who was asleep on the couch. When I got to my bedroom, I was greeted by a picture of Jaydene and Nate's funeral mass card that sat on my dresser. Tears welled up in my eyes. I flopped onto my bed and crumpled into the fetal position. I wanted all the pain to go away.

Over the coming weeks, I was an emotionless drone going through the meaningless routines of my broken life. I didn't care about anything. Most of all, I didn't care if I lived or died. I just wanted the pain to subside. I began hanging out in the back of the restaurant with the questionable kitchen guys. They usually doled stories of party mayhem, but they also doled something else I needed. Beatrice noticed me hanging with them. It was apparent she disapproved.

"Dude. You should have been at Joey's party. Mike was so drunk he tackled Joey, and they both went through the drywall. Classic," he said, flicking his cigarette.

"Yeah. I could have used the distraction. My life is a total cesspool right now," I said.

"I hear you. I've been nothin' but totally toasted since Nate died. My deal is... don't deal with it."

"If God existed, He surely wouldn't let people like Nate die like that. I can't handle this garbage anymore. I don't care about anything. Can you hook me up with something?"

"True that! I got something that will fix up you for sure." He shoved a couple of pills into my hand. "You're gonna love these. No pain and all to gain."

I smiled.

"You read my mind."

He handed me a flask filled with whiskey.

"I suggest downing them with a little of this, and you'll be flyin' in no time."

I downed the pills with a big swig of whiskey from the flask. They dulled the physical pain but didn't do much for my emotional scars. I took another big gulp of the whiskey.

"Easy dude. Save some for me," he said, grabbing the bottle out of my hands.

I staggered into the restaurant and did my best to keep my composure.

Beatrice tried to grab my attention.

"What's cookin', good lookin'? Cat got your tongue?"

I walked blankly past her.

"Well! I guess someone's gotta get the funk outta their truck," she exclaimed.

As I entered the kitchen, I pushed past Josie. She also noted my detached demeanor but didn't stop me. She joined Beatrice at the cash stand.

"Hey. I'm a bit concerned about our friend. He hasn't been himself for over a couple of months now...ever since Nate's funeral," Josie said in a hushed tone.

"Yeah...I think he's also dealing with some girl troubles too. You better keep an eye on him. I saw him out back with some of our favorite kitchen crew members. Looks like he's usin', too."

Beatrice gave her a stern look.

"Keep an eye on him!"

"Yeah...I'll do what I can," Josie replied.

At the end of my shift, the unrelenting pain was back in my heart. I needed more of the kitchen guy's remedy. I hung out in my car until he emerged for his cig break.

"Hey! You got more of those bad boys you gave me earlier?"

"Dude...I'm always stocked."

"How much?"

"Twenty bucks will set you up just fine."

I unfurled my tip money and handed it to him.

"Done deal. Here." He stealthily slipped a small baggie filled with pills into my waiting hand.

"If you really want to get toasted, I suggest a shot of whiskey with three of these."

"Way ahead of you, bro."

I slipped a bottle of whiskey out from under my jacket. I snatched it from the bar when the front area emptied out.

"Courtesy of the Red Mill bar," I said with delight.

The kitchen guy laughed. "Classic!"

I sat emotionless in my car. I watched traffic blankly while I downed several pills with repeated swigs of whiskey. When I finished the bottle of whiskey, I smashed it on the ground next to my car and drove off erratically. Somehow, I made it home and staggered into my house. I felt sick.

Clumsily, I passed his father, who was again asleep on the couch in the living room. As I stumbled by the kitchen, I caught a fuzzy my mother at the table watching the news on a small television. She was solemnly engrossed and didn't notice me.

I fumbled my way to my bedroom. When I saw a picture of myself with Jaydene, I thrashed it onto the floor. I picked up Nate's funeral mass card, crumpled it up, and threw it against the wall hitting the cross that hung there. Tears flowed down my cheeks like a river of sorrow. My pain remedy wasn't working. I rummaged through my dresser, pulled out a medicine bottle I swiped from our bathroom medicine cabinet. I also had a flask of whiskey I'd hidden there earlier that week. I popped some of the pills with a swig of whiskey. I flopped onto my bed in a dazed nauseous heap.

Thoughts of better times with Jaydene and my friend, Nate, raced through my mind only to be overtaken by our devastating breakup and the casket holding Nate's body. "Why would God put someone through all this pain?" I thought. "Why?"

A few days later, I scuttled my way into my house after a long day at work. My parents were standing in the kitchen, waiting for me. They both had stern disappointing looks washed across their faces. I glanced at them and made a feeble attempt to go to my bedroom. The half-empty bag of pills and a small whiskey bottle dangling from my mother's hands stopped me in my tracks.

"Can you tell me what you are doing with these?" she asked.

She was shaking in anger and disappointment.

"We didn't raise you for this," my father growled.

I raised my voice to a level I'd never used with my parents before. Anger pulsed through my veins, along with my shame.

"What the hell were you doing in my room? You were going through my things," I screamed.

"They were in your jacket pocket...in the wash! Can we even trust you anymore? I'm scared to death to go on vacation with your father next week."

My father was equally disappointed with me.

"How are we supposed to leave you here alone in this house?"

"Do what you want to me! I don't care. I don't care about anything anymore," I scoffed.

"Who do you think you're talking to, Mister? As long as you live in this house...*in my house*, you'll be respectful. Do you hear me?" my father roared.

"Maybe I shouldn't live here. You don't know me. No one does! You don't know what's going on with my garbage life. Just throw me away like everyone else has. This conversation is over."

I stormed off to my room and slammed the door. My father angrily moved forward, posturing himself for a fight. My mother grabbed his shoulder.

"Now, now, John. Just let him be. Just let him be," she soothed.

He backed down. I just laid there in my bed wallowing in my disgrace. My life was spiraling out of control, and I didn't know how to stop it.

***

The following week, I was alone in the house while my parents reluctantly went on their planned Caribbean cruise. I felt some peace having the house all to myself.

On my last night shift for the week, I arrived home to a dark house. I flicked on the television and slumped onto the couch. The eleven o'clock news was on. When I fumbled for the cable channel box, I suddenly saw Dylan's high school yearbook picture on the newscast.

"The body of the young man found dead yesterday morning at the Milton Hotel has been identified as nineteen-year-old Dylan Davidson. The County Sheriff's Office confirmed that Davidson died of a single self-inflicted gunshot wound. His family has not yet released a statement. Davidson was a recent graduate of Cromwell High School. In other news, stocks are expected to rebound after..."

I collapsed to my knees in an emotional heap. Rage and pain filled my soul.

"Why are you doing this to me, God? Why? Why? I can't take anymore! Do you hear me? I'm done," I shrieked.

I grabbed a bottle of scotch out of my parent's liquor cabinet and some pills I rummaged from our bathroom medicine cabinets. I took a handful of pills and downed them with a gulp from the bottle.

I emptied the liquor bottle in no time and collapsed onto my bed for a short time. I was going in and out of consciousness. The prescription medicine bottle dropped from my limp hand as I attempted to stand up. I pushed my way out of the house and into the wooded area that connected my street with Jaydene's neighborhood.

I started running through the woods. I didn't know what I was running from or what I was running to anymore. I just wanted to escape my life. I tripped over a branch. With a thud, I planted my face into the dirt. There was no pain, just the stale smell of death's earth. I didn't want to get up. I wanted to lie there and die. Somehow, I pushed myself back to my feet and kept going.

When I emerged into Jaydene's neighborhood, I staggered clumsily toward her house. I squeezed myself behind the shrubs next to her front door. My limp hand banged haphazardly on her bedroom window. It was my desperate cry for attention. It was my cry of desperation. I had nowhere else to go.

"Jay? Please...I...need you...I need..."

She was half awake when she slid her window open.

"What are you doing here? You can't be here."

My words were a blur.

"I...need you...I need..."

I fell back against the bushes, collapsing onto the ground in a dazed stupor.

"Oh, my God," she exclaimed.

She ran to me and tried to lift me. I was so woozy my feet only dragged behind me. Somehow, she guided me into her living room.

I struggled for my words.

"Jay...I...I...don't think I can...do this anymore...I can't..."

The room was a tilt-a-whirl. My voice wavered, and my legs suddenly gave out from under me. I crumpled into a dead heap, crashing my head against her dining room table. As my lifeless body fell before her, she could only scoop my head into her arms. Tears flowed down her face.

"No! Don't you die! Don't you die on me! Wake up! Please! Please!"

When I came to, she was frantically rocking my head and sobbing in utter agony.

My weakened voice scratched the morbid air that filled the room.

"I'm sorry. I...I...didn't mean to do this to you,"

The tears flowing down my ashen cheeks joined hers when she leaned her head into mine.

"Don't you close your eyes. You need to stay awake. You stay with me. Do you hear me?"

When the dawn's early light flashed across her living room, she was still holding my head in her arms. She saved my life by keeping me lucid that night. I know I hurt her emotionally with my antics. I carried that guilt in my heart for years. I always hoped that I helped her heal the scars of her mother's suicide in some way when she rescued my weary soul.

"I'm really worried about you, but I have to get you outta here before Nan wakes up. Do you think you can stand?"

I felt like I'd just spent a week in barren desert wasteland, clinging to life. My voice was dry and groggy.

"I think so. The spins stopped a while ago."

She grabbed my arm and helped me up.

"I'll drive you home, okay. You need to promise me you'll go get checked out today. You weren't moving when you fell. I thought you died. It so was awful. Don't you ever do that to me again."

"I'm sorry for everything, but I don't wanna see a doctor.

Just get me home. I'll be okay," I said.

She was torn.

"I can't leave you like this, but I..."

I feebly reassured. "It's okay. I'll be okay."

Barely a word was spoken in the car. We were both emotionally fried. Before she left me, I had to vow to her several times that I would go to a local urgent care. Instead, I dropped onto my couch from exhaustion. My mind was engulfed with a splitting headache and thoughts of how far I'd fallen. I had nothing but contempt for my reckless actions. A couple of hours later, I crawled my way to the kitchen phone to call in sick to work. When I stood up, the blood rushed out of my head. I had trouble dialing. My voice was shaky.

"Hey Beatrice. I'm not...uhhhh...feeling good. Tell Mr. Maiden I won't be in. Okay?"

"What's wrong with you? Are you on anything?"

"No. I'm just sick."

The concern in her voice grew.

"Are your parents there? Let me speak to them."

"No...they're away."

Her inquisition continued.

"Is your brother there?"

"No...he's not here either...it's okay...I'm...uhhhh..."

Everything suddenly went black.

I awoke in an ambulance with an IV drip hooked up to my

arm. I was strapped to a gurney flanked by two paramedics. They were less than enamored with me.

"I just don't understand why he would do this garbage to himself. They won't even pump his stomach. The chems are already in his bloodstream."

The other paramedic shook his head in displeasure.

"What are we, a glorified taxi service? I guess our friends at the medical center will just leave him out in the hallway to dry out with the other junkies."

"Another waste of our time, if you ask me. We could be out helping someone in real need." He turned toward me in disgust. "Instead we got one like this...and alas, here we are. Frustrating!"

He threw his arms into the air.

"C'est la vie."

His eyes narrowed at me.

"Wait. Isn't this Dave Clancy's brother?"

The other paramedic smirked.

"Oh, boy, is he gonna be pissed."

"I guess I'll call him."

"Better you than me."

I just stayed quiet and took their lamenting. They were right. I did this to myself. It was my choice. My stupid decision.

I was the only one to blame. The shame in my heart grew, and now it was bearing rotting fruit. I could no longer keep the lid on my Pandora's Box.

The paramedics wheeled me into the hospital hallway and then placed me into a wheelchair situated among a few detoxing junkies and drunks. A couple of hours later, my brother David approached the nurse's station. The attending nurse pointed me out to him.

His shadow loomed over me.

"Hey. What's goin' on?"

I averted eye contact.

"I'm sorry. I let you down. I let myself down. I let everyone down."

He slowly knelt next to me.

"Let's not talk about it."

"Are you gonna tell Mom and Pop?" I cowered.

I lifted my chin and was greeted by a small smile on his face.

"Hell, no. I'm just glad you're okay, and you're lucky I know those paramedics. They didn't check you in so there are no records of this."

"Really?"

"Yeah. Really. I know I always give you crap, but I really do care about you, and Karen is worried about you too."

My eyes darted to the floor.

"I know."

He placed his hand on my shoulder. "You're one of the best brothers I could ask for in this life."

"You are, too. You've always been there for me. I'm…I'm really lost."

"I know. I don't know how to fix you. I wish I did."

"I don't know how to fix me either…and you're really not gonna tell Mom and Pop?"

"Yeah…I won't…but consider us even for that time you covered for me when I stayed at Karen Meyer's house all night."

A half-smile appeared on my face.

"She was kinda nasty, you know."

He put his arm around me. "Don't push your luck, Shrimp. Come on, let's get you home."

After a few days of rest, I pulled myself together and went back to work. When I arrived at the Red Mill parking lot, suddenly I saw Jaydene with Danny standing at the far end of the lot. I stepped out of my car, and she ran over to me.

"I'm really scared. You can't do this to yourself. I don't want to lose you. I care about you. I do, and he does too, but…" She peered back at Danny for a moment. "I know things have changed between us, but I'll always…you know…"

"Jay, you don't have to do this. I know you care about me. You always have."

Her voice lowered as she placed her hand on my heart.

"I just want you to know, that's all. Maybe we…"

"It's okay. It's me. It's my fault. I'm broken. I'm just dying inside. I just want all the pain to go away. If I could change things I would—us…Nate…Dylan…all of it…but I just have to live with it somehow, and I don't know if I can. I'm trying. I'm so sorry I hurt you, I just..."

She placed her finger on my lips and pulled me in for a momentary hug before returning to Danny. When she reached him, he took her hand. As they walked away, she turned and shared a small nod with me.

It was the first olive branch my heart ever received, and I needed it. I was at the door of the darkest place my life had ever been. At the time, I knew only one thing about rock bottom—the black hopelessness that consumes you. I was soon to discover the other thing you'll find there— the way out. You just have to lift your weary chin and look up toward the light that's always shining down upon precious soul. I had to find a way to climb.

Death comes in many forms—the loss of a loved one, a complete change in your life, or your demise. The one great takeaway on death is that it's never an end, but rather the seed for a new beginning. This cycle of life is how renewal is created. With every death, the seeds of rebirth are planted, and love always helps those seeds grow. Love is stronger than death, even though it can't stop this destruction from happening. Death can never separate you from love.

FIFTEEN
THE MESSENGER

"Of all the challenges you've faced, you can only
be made better for them. Just as all the great
masterworks of art have weathered the wrath of
time, only to become more revered in their inherent
beauty, you, too, are counted among them in the
hearts of the angels."

— Robert Clancy

The delicate wings of an angel are made from the fabric of glistening hope and sewn together with the light of compassion. That's why you are meant to glide in this life on the celestial winds of love. Every act of kindness matters, no matter how small and insignificant it may seem. A kind word or loving message is worth more to the recipient than your beautiful heart will ever know. Never underestimate the power of compassion.

A week or so after my big downfall, I was still struggling with everything. I tried my best to go through the motions of daily life. I would do anything to seem normal, but my Pandora's box had been opened for all to see. One night at the

189

end of my work shift, I spun around to leave, and I found Josie standing behind me. There was a kindness in her eyes I hadn't seen before. She placed her hands on my shoulders.

"Hey. I need to talk to you," she said softly.

"What about?"

Her voice lowered. "I know what you're doing."

"What?"

"I know what you're doing to yourself, and you need to stop, or you're gonna end up killing yourself."

I tried to evade. "I'm not doing..."

Her gaze narrowed. "I know."

Her eyes had a loving look that only your mother could give you. Tears immediately welled up in my eyes. I broke down.

"I just don't want this pain anymore. I don't want to live with this. I just can't."

"Listen, I've been there, and I know how you feel inside. I do. My mother died in my arms. I wouldn't wish that on anyone... and I've been through tougher times than that...but I made it through."

She held out her hand with her palm facing up. "Put your hand out like this," she commanded.

I obeyed while she rummaged through her purse and pulled out a small tri-fold pamphlet. She placed it in my outstretched hand as she rested her hand on top of it.

"This got me through some difficult times, and I want you to go home, say a prayer and do this tonight," she said.

As she removed her hand from mine, she revealed a pamphlet. It was titled "A Christian's Guide to Prayerful Meditation."

She grabbed my shoulders again and looked intently into my eyes. "I know you'll find peace if you do this. I know in my heart this will help you."

I melted into her arms for a loving hug as tears of hope dripped from my cheeks. "Thank you, Josie. I'll try. I will."

She held me a bit tighter. "I care about you. I really do."

I went straight home, sat on the edge of my bed, and read the pamphlet cover to cover. After reviewing a couple of more times through, I set it aside and flicked off the light. I prayed quietly to myself for a moment as instructed in the booklet, but anger and pain I'd been harboring could not be contained. I clenched my fists. I challenged God.

"If there's a God, I need to see something tonight with my own eyes, or I'm done! Do you hear me?" I commanded as I raised my fists. "And if you exist...heal me. So have at it! You got that? This is my last night. I'm done!"

I fell back onto my bed, and closed my eyes, asked for God's mercy. I began reciting the 'Our Father' prayer over and over to myself. At one point, I even tried to imagine what Jesus looked like—every line of His face—every whisker in His beard.

Around 3 am, I thought I saw a gentle pulsing light with

what the booklet described as my "mind's eye," and it broke my peaceful concentration. I opened my eyes to find a bright, laser-pointer-like white light twinkling on my wall near the edge of the ceiling. I wrinkled my brow and crossed my arms. "I thought I was having *an experience*. It's just a stupid light shining through my window," I seethed.

Even so, this light seemed different. It was centered within a dark oval shadow that appeared to be a black hole on my wall. The room was filled with an ethereal luminance.

I leaped up from the bed and moved my window curtain to stop the light. It didn't. *"The light must be coming from a reflection off my watch or something."* But I couldn't find the source. The beam could not be broken, not even when I waved my hand in front of it. *"The light is coming from the wall."* I was baffled.

I sat back on the edge of my bed. 'This is weird,' I thought, glancing at the pamphlet. 'Now what?'

The light was mesmerizing. I couldn't take my eyes off it. It looked like a tiny shimmering star. The dark oval area slowly increased in size as the light intensified. It even seemed to morph at one point into a small angelic shape. It reminded me of a paper cutout of an angel. I smiled. *"Now this is getting interesting. The book didn't mention this part."*

Suddenly, the light flashed and opened like a butterfly coming out of its cocoon. I saw a Barbie doll-sized angelic figure coming toward the small hole on my wall. Time seemed to slow down. I rubbed my eyes, dropped my hands to my side, and exclaimed, *"Oh, my God!"*

At my annunciation, the dark oval enlarged to the size of the wall, and the angel emerged into my room. I lost all sense of time as heavenly peace washed over my soul.

My thoughts raced at the sight of the visage. She had the most divine face I'd ever seen, beyond all the paintings and books I'd come across in my life—a pure, classic beauty. She was larger than a human—approximately six-and-a-half to seven feet tall, adorned in a thin, white robe, a simple braided rope around her waist, a delicate tiara seated on her head, and plain sandals wrapped her feet—exactly what you'd expect, but more.

I could feel only pure love radiating through my body within her presence. The whole figure was ghost-like, shimmering white, and semi-transparent—almost as if she was made of light. She exuded a nobleness that made me feel like I was in the presence of royalty. Her wings were shaped like those of a dove, and her hair gracefully curled around her celestial face.

I was awed by the size and beauty of her wings. The perfectly formed wings stretched out nearly four feet from each of her shoulders. I focused on the details of every feather intimately as she slowly floated forward, meeting me nose to nose.

I leaned back was slightly cross-eyed, trying to keep focused on her beautiful face. Although there was no physical touch, she greeted me with a momentary kiss before backing up. I felt a love in my heart like no other I'd ever experienced in my life when she greeted me. Taking in the whole vision, instantly she reminded me of a quintessential Greek or Roman statue. She was a saintly goddess.

Here I was, simple me, face to face with one of God's

supreme messengers. I felt loving warmth throughout my body. When I closed my eyes, in my mind's eye, I could see that she was emitting a celestial light that fell upon me.

I felt healing.

At that moment, I realized fuzzily that I could have asked any of the questions you seem to always ask about God and creation.

What's the purpose of life?

What happens when we die?

Do we have past lives?

What's a soul?

Does hell exist?

Instead of asking a question of profound import, I straightened my back, shrugged my shoulders, and raised my hands out in front of me, almost in disbelief. "So, what are we doing here?" Not exactly my brightest moment.

So simple. So human.

I surveyed the life I had created for myself in this moment of moments, and I was way off the course I was placed here on Earth to follow. I knew I was engulfed in negativity, but now I could see how to transcend it and help others do the same. She showed me.

Although she didn't speak, somehow I had the sense that she could read my mind. I tested this theory by thinking of a corny joke. '*What did the boy bear say to the girl bear on Valentine's Day? I love you beary much!*' Another one of my stellar moments.

194

She half-smiled just like the Mona Lisa, which, in turn, made me smile and snicker.

"So you can read my mind." She blinked and nodded in affirmation.

While I marveled at the thought that I just made an angel smile, the light of the universe began radiating from her. My entire body, every fiber of my being, was suddenly at complete peace—beyond love, beyond happiness—just peace. It was as if I was being hit with a gentle pulsing light made from pure unconditional love. My soul was healed. "This is what heaven is. This is what God is."

I closed my eyes, and from my mind's eye, I saw an x-ray-like outline of the angel with spiraling light emitting from her body onto my chest. I breathed in and exuded a peaceful sigh. I was filled with peace. I was beyond love...just total peace. I didn't want it to end.

The angel stayed in the same position for nearly the entire encounter. I thought, 'Are you going to say something?' No words were ever spoken. Instead, I swarmed with new thoughts. I knew her name, "Gabriel." She conveyed, "This is the form I have chosen that is most comfortable for you. Never have fear, doubt or worry again."

The heavenly light continued to pour into my body, and slowly, she lifted her hand with the index finger extended. While watching this movement unfold, I was suddenly reminded of the outstretched "hand of God" painted on the ceiling of the Sistine Chapel by Michelangelo. She reached out and gently touched my forehead between my eyes, opening my mind to all of the love in the universe.

Gently, I closed my eyes and lost all sense of time. My body grew warmer as thousands of spiritual messages began rapidly flowing into me. The messages came to me in the form of pictures from a flickering slideshow and thoughts from elsewhere that permeated my mind. It was as if my thoughts and another's were merged into one.

I wasn't on my planned life path. I was supposed to be helping people. I had a purpose to fulfill, and I needed to move away from the detrimental and destructive course I was on.

It's all up to me.

I have a choice.

I always had a choice.

Never have fear again.

I am healed.

While Divine messages swirled around in my head, the angel gradually floated away from me into the enlarged portal. Her figure slowly diminished as the distance between us grew, but she never stopped smiling at me. Her light became a single focused point, and then it was gone.

I sat in astonishment for a few minutes, shook my head, and ran to the bathroom to look at myself in the mirror. For some reason, I needed to see my face. I jumped off the bed and ran to the bathroom. I placed my hands on the bathroom counter and stared at my reflection in the mirror.

"I need to have a conversation with you. You're the only one who is ever gonna believe you." I pointed at myself and nodded. "Dude, that just happened! *You know now!* You *know* God exists!"

"Why me?" I frowned and pointed my thumb into my chest.

"Why you?" I answered.

The gravity of the situation started to sink in. "You can't tell anyone about this... they'll think you're crazy. You'll be put into a straitjacket!" I waved my finger at my reflection. "No! You have to keep this to yourself. You'll just have to live with knowing. You're the only one who is ever going to believe you."

A smile grew on my face, "She showed you that you're not on your path. You're here to teach love and kindness...to work with youth. How do you know that? You just know?" I was in awe. "You know heaven is real... you're gonna have to live with this knowledge for the rest of your days. Your life is changed forever...you have to change...*everything has changed.*"

I continued to interrogate my reflection. I asked a question to which I already knew the answer. *"So, what are you going to do with this?"* I knew all the answers were already within me, and other answers would unfold consciously when I was ready for them.

It was all in my hands now. My life. My love. It all had a new meaning.

I felt so alone, yet paradoxically, I felt connected to everyone and everything at the same time. I no longer feared death, and I was somehow completely renewed with the precious gift of pure love and wanting to live the rest of my life in that love.

I ran out into my front yard to rejoice. I had to see the stars. My arms outstretched toward the heavens. I was smiling from ear to ear looking up at the precious flickering lights dancing across the night sky. I wanted to tell the whole world, "God is real! Heaven is real!" I wanted to scream this message at the top of my lungs. Instead, I just held it all in my heart.

I didn't even tell my own family about this celestial encounter until 2012, nearly thirty years later. It was the night my mother was on her deathbed. At the nursing home, where both of my parents were cared for, I asked my siblings if I could take my father back to his room. I struggled at first to get my words out to him.

I raised my hand to my chin and darted my eyes to the floor. "I've tried to do my best. I have, Pop. You know that. You've seen the volunteer work I do. I've tried to be kinder to others, but I'm not perfect. No one is. We're all flawed, and that's the beauty of life. Right, Pop?"

He nodded.

I took a deep breath and shared my angelic encounter with him. When I finished, his stoic face didn't change. I could only hope he understood everything I said.

I paused for another minute in silence and then asked a staff member to bring my father something to eat. Before I departed, I sat next to him and said, "We'll all be together again on the other side, and Mom will be waiting for us. I know it."

He nodded again slightly, perhaps in agreement. I hugged him and stood up. "Goodnight, Pop. I love you."

He raised his thumb. "You, too."

Later that night, my mother crossed over into the waiting arms of the angels. It was Mother's Day. That morning she was celebrated in a Mass of the Blessed Virgin Mary, the greatest mother of all. *How beautiful!*

When you join the human race, it feels like you're continually running along with the shadows of doubt and fear, but in reality, you're always heading toward the light. You get there by taking a momentary pause to look at that luminous point on the horizon. You're never alone in your race—you're always held in God's hands while all the angels hold yours along the way. The race is never-ending, but you can win by merely believing in love.

SIXTEEN
REVERIE

*"After every disaster, long winter or terrible
storm, renewal is written into the very fabric
of nature itself. This process begins the second
the storm subsides. This resilience is also
written into the fabric of your soul.
Your resilience is how you truly shine."*

— Robert Clancy

Loss is not the end—it's the beginning of a new, beautiful chapter, and no matter what, you need to try with all your heart to begin it with love! I've thought about the angel every single day of my life since that encounter. I've deeply pondered all the gifts she bestowed upon me, and the one thing she took from me—faith. It seems odd that I've lost faith, but faith for me is a trust in something you're not sure exists. I'm sure. My faith was replaced with unequivocal belief.

The next day I set out on a journey to find my way back to my life path but knowing your pathway in life is only half the equation. You need to walk it with all the faith, hope, and love you can carry. Love is the reason for your being. Hope gives you the courage to rise above every adversity. Faith is the compass that guides you back to that divine love. When you truly open your heart, you not only allow all the light in, but you also gain the angelic ability to release its precious message to the world.

A beautiful quote by French writer and poet Alphonse de Lamartine quintessentially explains this kind of divine love. He wrote, *"To love for the sake of being loved is human, but to love for the sake of loving is angelic."* Yes. You just need to love for love's precious sake—what a fantastic way to go through life!

Divine love is like a precious spiral from which your entire universe was created. It has a definitive beginning, retains its original form as it grows, forever spreading light to all it touches. I set out to create those ripples in the universe.

Within the eleven years following my divine encounter, I'd dedicated myself to volunteering and helping young people. I met my soulmate and future wife, Lauren, at my brother's wedding in the spring of 1988. We married in the fall of 1990. Lauren and I were blessed with the arrival of our precious son Sean in the fall of 1999. Jaydene later met and married the perfect husband. She is an incredible mother and role model to two amazing sons. Everything always works out just the way it's meant to do when you surrender to it.

After my divine encounter, I tried to be a better, kinder, and more compassionate person. My journey wasn't always easy or pleasant, but I kept putting one foot in front of the other to try to reach every one of those celestial summits.

It's true that the further you climb, the further you have to fall, but aren't those incredibly beautiful views worth the risk? You should never underestimate what you're capable of accomplishing with love! You're a precious soul who deserves to bask in the light of those summits! Keep climbing.

In the mid 1990's, I stepped up to be the chair of The New York East Youth Leadership (HOBY) conference. HOBY's mission is to inspire and prepare future young leaders for a life dedicated to leadership, service, and innovation. This organization empowers young people to dream big, make an impact, and change the world in profoundly positive ways. I started volunteering with this beautiful group shortly after my divine encounter. I was guided to do this.

There were hundreds of high school sophomores, parents, and seminar staff leaders heading into a college campus auditorium for the closing ceremony. My mind was swimming over my closing speech. There was a tsunami of people flooding into the hall, and I was lost.

"I don't have a message! What am I going to say to all of them?"

The students and seminar staff were enthusiastic and cheering as they moved into the building. I was walking with Stephanie and Dan, two of the late-teenaged student staff members.

Stephanie glanced over her shoulder at me and smiled.

"What are you going to say for your keynote speech? Are you nervous? There's gonna be like seven hundred people in there."

"Hmmmm...I'm not exactly sure what I'll say yet. I keep blanking out."

I pointed to my heart. "I guess I'll just have to let this speak. It's the greatest voice you have—the one that's louder than any words can ever be."

Dan placed his hand on my shoulder. "I hope you know you're one of the most inspirational people I've ever met."

"I respect that, but no. I just do what I can to make a difference."

"No. You are! I really mean that."

"I uh..."

We were suddenly interrupted by a group of cheering students. "Hey...It's the B-O-B!!! How do you spell Bob?" Their cheers grew louder. "B-O-B! How do you spell Bob backwards? B-O-B! We love you B-O-B!"

The group continued cheering for me as they headed off toward the closing ceremony. I was slighting embarrassed over the attention. Parents of one of the students stopped us after witnessing the cheer.

"You seem to be kinda a big deal here," the father announced. "I don't think I've ever witnessed this many smiles in one place. Can you tell me where we're supposed to go for the closing ceremony?"

"I just show up for the fireworks," I said, trying to divert the attention away from myself. "The closing ceremony is right through those doors over there, then go to the left down the hallway. We have staff in there to assist you...and they'll be smiling...*guaranteed.*"

He took his wife's hand. "Wonderful! We'll see you in there."

"See what I mean? You just make everyone so happy," Dan said.

A smile appeared on my face. "A while back, I learned that to really be happy, you need to understand that your smile is one of the greatest gifts you can share with someone. When you give everything in your heart, it's instantly refilled with twice as much as you gave. That is the beauty of life and why it's worth living. Never underestimate how precious your soul is. Every act of kindness you do truly does matter."

"So true...so true. You are just filled with so much wisdom. That's what I love about you," Stephanie chimed.

I reflected for a moment. "That's what they keep telling me, but honestly, I have to give credit to an angel who showed up for me at just the right time with just the right message. I made a promise to myself that day that I would try to do better—that I would try to *be better*. I've just done the best I could since then."

Dan's smile grew and his eyes lit up with enthusiasm.

"You've certainly shown us how to do that, and I know I speak for Stephanie when I say this, but we can't wait to introduce you today."

Stephanie winked at Dan. "Yep...Dan and I have something special planned. Let's just say you've been an angel for all of us."

"Hey! No surprises, guys. Please don't do anything special for me."

"Too late for that!" Dan exclaimed.

I shook my head.

A short time later, I was waiting offstage to be introduced for my closing ceremony keynote speech. Dan and Stephanie approached the podium.

"Hi! I'm Dan Dwyer, and it gives me great pleasure to introduce Robert 'B-O-B' Clancy. He's not only been a volunteer with our organization for over ten years..." He glanced back at me and shared a smile. "But he is someone I can truly call one of my heroes. He's led us all by example on how one person can make a difference by simply giving what's in his heart."

Stephanie leaned into the mic. "Hello everyone! I'm Stephanie Carson. I would just like to add that Mr. Clancy is someone I consider a true angel...so...a few of us sneaked off campus last night cuz we needed to get a few supplies."

A small group of students stepped out from behind the curtain holding up two sizeable makeshift angel wings made from cardboard covered with aluminum foil.

Dan took a glass and spoon out from within the podium and began to ring it into the mic. "I heard something about a bell ringing and an angel getting its wings." He looked over his shoulder at me. "So it looks like this guy just earned his."

The crowd erupted in cheers. I walked toward the podium, deeply humbled to give my message, but it had already been delivered.

"Love has no boundaries; thus it can never be conquered. Love has no walls; thus it is always open. Love has no limits; thus it has no end."

Supporting Others

"Volunteers may be the ones who give of their time,
but they're always the ones who make time
to give all their hearts."

— *Robert Clancy*

The author supports the New York East Hugh O'Brian Youth Leadership Seminar, which fosters youth leadership through community service and Junior Achievement of Northeastern New York, an organization that inspires and prepares young people for work readiness, entrepreneurship, and financial literacy through the use of experiential, hands-on programs.

Inspiring, Educational, Compassionate,

Energizing, Enthusiastic, Motivating, Transforming,

Long-Lasting, and Life-Changing

These are some of the words that students, schools, parents, alumni, volunteers, and supporters use to describe Hugh O'Brian Youth Leadership (HOBY).

Founded in 1958, HOBY's mission is to inspire and develop our global community of youth and volunteers to a life dedicated to leadership, service, and innovation. HOBY programs are conducted annually throughout the United States, serving local and international high school students.

The New York East Leadership Seminar provides youth in eastern New York a unique three-day motivational leadership training, service learning, and motivation-building experience. New York East HOBY also provides adults with opportunities to make a significant impact on the lives of youth by volunteering.

NYE Hugh O'Brian Youth Leadership Seminar
77 Old Glenham Road
Glenham, NY 12527
www.hobynye.org

About the Author

"If you truly want to hear the angels sing, just listen quietly to the love songs performed by the magnificence within your heart."

— *Robert Clancy*

Robert Clancy is a creative visionary, #1 international bestselling author, spiritual teacher, Christian minister and co-founder of Spiral Design. At age nineteen, Robert had a divine spiritual experience with one of God's angels that altered his life in profound ways—something he kept a close secret for nearly thirty years of his life. In 2012, he created the Robert Clancy – Guide to the Soul Facebook fan page, where he shares his divinely inspired thoughts, now followed by nearly one million people worldwide.

He is a sought-after speaker, presenter, and guest. Robert is a regular contributor and weekly guest on Los Angeles KABC Radio's syndicated *Late Night Health Radio Show*. He's also co-host and producer of *The Mindset Reset Show* (MindsetResetTV.com), which has hosted notable guests such as the star of the hit film, *The Secret*, Dr. Joe Vitale, actor Kevin Sorbo, actress Dee Wallace, Arielle Ford, and Marci Shimoff among others. His latest book *Soul Cyphers: Decoding a Life of Hope and Happiness* quickly became a #1 international bestseller.

Robert is also a featured spiritual expert appearing with Dr. Joe Vitale, don Miguel Ruiz, Brian Tracy and Dannion Brinkley in the movie *Becoming the Keys*, set to release in early 2019. Robert also recently completed his filming of an episode for the 2018 season of the Emmy® Award-winning *Dr. Nandi Show* which reaches over 300 million people on major cable and satellite television networks such as Discovery and ABC.

As early as age six, Robert had immense compassion for humanity. He commits his life to assisting others, whether volunteering, helping them to succeed, or even just offering a friendly smile. Robert is a husband, father, and 6th Degree Master Black Belt martial arts instructor.

Connect with Robert at:

GuideToTheSoul.com

TheMessengerMovies.com

MindsetResetTV.com

SpiralDesign.com

Facebook.com/GuideTotheSoul

YouTube.com/GuideToTheSoul

Twitter.com/GuideToSoul

Instagram.com/GuideToTheSoul

SPEAKING OPPORTUNITIES

"Your heart speaks louder than
your voice ever could."

— *Robert Clancy*

Robert Clancy's compelling speaking engagements, keynotes, and seminars are now available for your event, company or organization!

In his signature keynote speeches, Decoding a Masterful Life and Leadership from the Heart, Robert uses examples from his books, *The Messenger*, *Soul Cyphers* and *The Hitchhiker's Guide to the Soul*, to learn how to improve your leadership through a compassion for others. Gain a sense of renewed purpose and self-worth. Realize the importance of your connection to humanity and how it enhances your career and life—every day.

Discover the exceptional power of kindness and the unexpected opportunities it provides to those who dare to give.

For all inquiries please contact us at:

Guide to the Soul
135 Mohawk Street
Cohoes, NY 12047

Phone: (518) 326-1135
email: inquiries@guidetothesoul.com
www.guidetothesoul.com

YOUR TIME TO SHINE

*"You come from the stardust as a reminder that
you always have the ability to shine even
in life's darkest moments."*

— *Robert Clancy*

I would love to hear from you about your life-changing volunteer experiences and your reaction to this book. If there was a particular story that added meaning to your life, please let me know how it affected you.

Please send your feedback to:

GuideToTheSoul.com/contact

or

share on Facebook @ facebook.com/guidetothesoul

I truly hope you enjoyed reading this book and that it inspires you choose a life path of compassion, grace, healing, happiness, peace, and unconditional love.

Made in the USA
Columbia, SC
24 January 2021

31500496R00117